By Leonard Woolf

History and Politics
INTERNATIONAL GOVERNMENT
EMPIRE AND COMMERCE IN AFRICA
CO-OPERATION AND THE FUTURE OF INDUSTRY
SOCIALISM AND CO-OPERATION
FEAR AND POLITICS
IMPERIALISM AND CIVILIZATION
AFTER THE DELUGE VOL. I
AFTER THE DELUGE VOL. II
QUACK, QUACK!
PRINCIPIA POLITICA
BARBARIANS AT THE GATE
THE WAR FOR PEACE

Criticism
HUNTING THE HIGHBROW
ESSAYS ON LITERATURE, HISTORY AND POLITICS

Fiction
THE VILLAGE IN THE JUNGLE
STORIES OF THE EAST
THE WISE VIRGINS

Drama
THE HOTEL

Autobiography
SOWING: AN AUTOBIOGRAPHY OF THE YEARS 1880 TO 1904
GROWING: AN AUTOBIOGRAPHY OF THE YEARS 1904 TO 1911
BEGINNING AGAIN: AN AUTOBIOGRAPHY OF THE YEARS 1911 TO 1918
DOWNHILL ALL THE WAY: AN AUTOBIOGRAPHY OF THE YEARS 1919 TO 1939
THE JOURNEY NOT THE ARRIVAL MATTERS:
AN AUTOBIOGRAPHY OF THE YEARS 1939 TO 1969

A CALENDAR OF CONSOLATION: A COMFORTING
THOUGHT FOR EVERY DAY IN THE YEAR

GROWING

AN AUTOBIOGRAPHY
OF THE YEARS 1904 TO 1911

Leonard Woolf

A Harvest Book
HARCOURT BRACE JOVANOVICH
NEW YORK AND LONDON

Printed in the United States of America

Library of Congress Cataloging in Publication Data
Woolf, Leonard Sidney, 1880-1969.
    Growing.
  (A Harvest book ; HB 320)
  Continuation of Sowing: an autobiography of the years 1880
to 1904. Continued by Beginning again; an autobiography of the
years 1911 to 1918.
  Includes index.
  1. Woolf, Leonard Sidney, 1880-1969. 2. Ceylon—Description
and travel. I. Title.
JA94.W6A28 1975 320'.092'4 [B] 75-9832
ISBN 0-15-637215-0

BCDEFGHIJ

CONTENTS

ILLUSTRATIONS

(*between pages 96 and 97*)

The author in Jaffna

Fisherman on Jaffna lagoon

Jaffna Hindu temple

Pearl Fishery: Arab divers with nose clips

Pearl Fishery: Preparing to dive

Pearl Fishery: Boats arriving from the banks

Pearl Fishery: Carrying the oysters into the koddu

The Empress Eugénie

*The author with the Ratemahatmayas outside the
    Kandy kachcheri*

Fetching water from the tank of a village in the jungle
    BY THE COURTESY OF ANGELA DAUGHARTY

*The author with Hambantota kachcheri staff, mudaliyars,
    muhandiram, and Engelbrecht*

*The author with Hambantota kachcheri staff and
    Father Cooreman*

MAPS

Si le roi m'avoit donné
    Paris sa grand'ville
Et qu'il me fallût quitter
    L'amour de ma vie!
Je dirois au roi Henri
    Reprenez votre Paris;
J'aime mieux ma vie, o gué!
    J'aime mieux ma mie.

FOREWORD

I HAVE tried in the following pages to tell the truth, the whole truth, and nothing but the truth, but of course I have not succeeded. I do not think that I have anywhere deliberately manipulated or distorted the truth into untruth, but I am sure that one sometimes does this unconsciously. In autobiography—or at any rate in my autobiography—distortion of truth comes frequently from the difficulty of remembering accurately the sequence of events, the temporal perspective. I have several times been surprised and dismayed to find that a letter or diary proves that what I remember as happening in, say, 1908 really happened in 1910; and the significance of the event may be quite different if it happened in the one year and not in the other. I have occasionally invented fictitious names for the real people about whom I write; I have only done so where they are alive or may be alive or where I think that their exact identification might cause pain or annoyance to their friends or relations. I could not have remembered accurately in detail fifty per cent of the events recorded in the following pages if I had not been able to read the letters which I wrote to Lytton Strachey and the official diaries which I had to write daily from 1908 to 1911 when I was Assistant Government Agent in the Hambantota District. I have to thank James Strachey for allowing me to read the original letters. As regards the diaries, I am greatly indebted to the Ceylon Government, particularly to the Governor, Sir Oliver Goonetilleke, and to Mr. Shelton C. Fernando of the Ceylon Civil Service, Secretary to the Ministry of Home

Affairs. When I visited Ceylon in 1960, Mr. Fernando, on behalf of the Ceylon Government, presented me with a copy of these diaries and the Governor subsequently gave orders that they should be printed and published.

Chapter One

THE VOYAGE OUT

In October 1904, I sailed from Tilbury Docks in the P. & O. *Syria* for Ceylon. I was a Cadet in the Ceylon Civil Service. To make a complete break with one's former life is a strange, frightening, and exhilarating experience. It has upon one, I think, the effect of a second birth. When one emerges from one's mother's womb one leaves a life of dim security for a world of violent difficulties and dangers. Few, if any, people ever entirely recover from the trauma of being born, and we spend a lifetime unsuccessfully trying to heal the wound, to protect ourselves against the hostility of things and men. But because at birth consciousness is dim and it takes a long time for us to become aware of our environment, we do not feel a sudden break, and adjustment is slow, lasting indeed a lifetime. I can remember the precise moment of my second birth. The umbilical cord by which I had been attached to my family, to St. Paul's, to Cambridge and Trinity was cut when, leaning over the ship's taffrail, I watched through the dirty, dripping murk and fog of the river my mother and sister waving good-bye and felt the ship begin slowly to move down the Thames to the sea.

To be born again in this way at the age of 24 is a strange experience which imprints a permanent mark upon one's character and one's attitude to life. I was leaving in England everyone and everything I knew; I was going to a place and life in which I really had not the faintest idea of how I should live and what I should be doing. All that I was taking with me from the old life as a contribution to the new and to prepare me for my task of helping to rule the British Empire was 90 large, beautifully printed volumes of Voltaire[1] and a wire-haired fox-terrier. The first impact of the new life was menacing and depressing. The ship slid down the oily dark waters of the river through cold clammy mist and rain; next day in the Channel it was barely possible to distinguish the cold and gloomy sky from the cold and gloomy sea. Within the boat there was the uncomfortable atmosphere of suspicion and reserve which is at first invariably the result when a number of English men and women, strangers to one another, find that they have to live together for a time in a train, a ship, a hotel.

In those days it took, if I remember rightly, three weeks to sail from London to Colombo. By the time we reached Ceylon, we had developed from a fortuitous concourse of isolated human atoms into a complex community with an elaborate system of castes and classes. The initial suspicion and reserve had soon given place to intimate friendships, intrigues, affairs, passionate loves and hates. I learned a great deal from my three weeks on board the P. & O. *Syria*. Nearly all my fellow-passengers were quite unlike the people whom I had known at home or at Cambridge. On the face of it and of them they were very ordinary persons with whom in my previous life I would have felt that I had little in common except perhaps mutual contempt. I learned two valuable lessons: first how to get on with ordinary persons, and secondly that there are practically no ordinary persons, that beneath the façade of John Smith and Jane Brown there is a strange character and often a passionate individual.

[1] The 1784 edition printed in Baskerville type.

THE VOYAGE OUT

One of the most interesting and unexpected exhibits was Captain L. of the Manchester Regiment, who, with a wife and small daughter, was going out to India. When I first saw and spoke to him, in the arrogant ignorance of youth and Cambridge, I thought he was inevitably the dumb and dummy figure which I imagined to be characteristic of any captain in the Regular Army. Nothing could have been more mistaken. He and his wife and child were in the cabin next to mine, and I became painfully aware that the small girl wetted her bed and that Captain L. and his wife thought that the right way to cure her was to beat her. I had not at that time read *A Child is being Beaten* or any other of the works of Sigmund Freud, but the hysterical shrieks and sobs which came from the next cabin convinced me that beating was not the right way to cure bed-wetting, and my experience with dogs and other animals had taught me that corporal punishment is never a good instrument of education.

Late one night I was sitting in the smoking-room talking to Captain L. and we seemed suddenly to cross the barrier between formality and intimacy. I took my life in my hands and boldly told him that he was wrong to beat his daughter. We sat arguing about this until the lights went out, and next morning to my astonishment he came up to me and told me that I had convinced him and that he would never beat his daughter again. One curious result was that Mrs. L. was enraged with me for interfering and pursued me with bitter hostility until we finally parted for ever at Colombo.

After this episode I saw a great deal of the captain. I found him to be a man of some intelligence and of intense intellectual curiosity, but in his family, his school, and his regiment the speculative mind or conversation was un-

known, unthinkable. He was surprised and delighted to
find someone who would talk about anything and everything, including God, sceptically. We found a third companion with similar tastes in the Chief Engineer, a dour
Scot, who used to join us late at night in the smoking-
room with two candles so that we could go on talking and
drinking whisky and soda after the lights went out. The
captain had another characteristic, shared by me: he had
a passion for every kind of game. During the day we
played the usual deck games, chess, draughts, and even
noughts and crosses, and very late at night when the two
candles in the smoking-room began to gutter, he would
say to me sometimes: "And now, Woolf, before the
candles go out, we'll play the oldest game in the world",
the oldest game in the world, according to him, being
a primitive form of draughts which certain arrangements
of stones, in Greenland and African deserts, show was
played all over the world by prehistoric man.

The three weeks which I spent on the P. & O. *Syria*
had a considerable and salutary effect upon me. I found
myself able to get along quite well in this new, entirely
strange, and rather formidable world into which I had
projected myself. I enjoyed adjusting myself to it and to
thirty or forty complete strangers. It was fascinating to
explore the minds of some and watch the psychological or
social antics of others. I became great friends with some
and even managed to have a fairly lively flirtation with a
young woman which, to my amusement, earned me a long,
but very kindly, warning and good advice from one of the
middle-aged ladies. The importance of that kind of voyage
for a young man with the age and experience or inexperi-
ence which were then mine is that the world and society
of the boat are a microcosm of the macrocosm in which

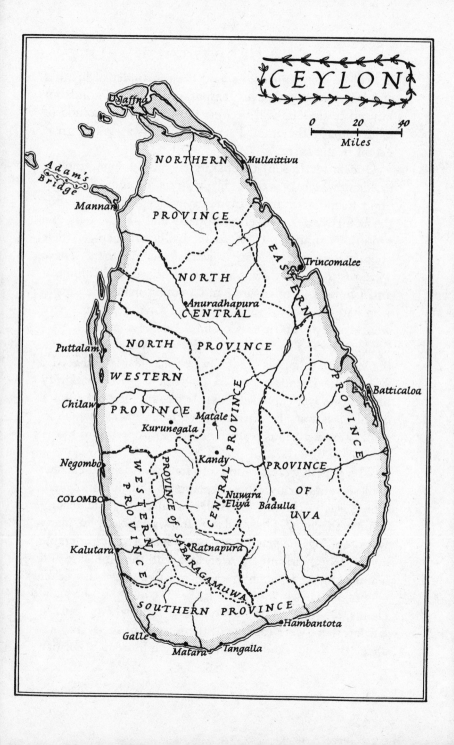

CEYLON

0   20   40
Miles

D. Jaffna

Adam's
Bridge

Mannar

NORTHERN   Mullaittivu

PROVINCE

NORTH   EASTERN

Anuradhapura   Trincomalee

CENTRAL

NORTH   PROVINCE

Puttalam

WESTERN   PROVINCE

Chilaw   Batticaloa

PROVINCE   Matale

Kurunegala

Kandy   PROVINCE

Negombo   CENTRAL PROVINCE   OF

COLOMBO   WESTERN PROVINCE   Nuwara   UVA
                                                Eliya   Badulla

Kalutara   Ratnapura
                PROVINCE of SABARAGAMUWA

                SOUTHERN   PROVINCE

                                        Hambantota
Galle
        Matara   Tangalla

he will be condemned to spend the remainder of his life, and it is probable that his temporary method of adjusting himself to the one will become the permanent method of adjustment to the other. I am sure that it was so to a great extent in my case.

One bitter lesson, comparatively new to me, and an incident which graved it deeply into my mind are still vivid to me after more than fifty years. I am still, after those fifty years, naïvely surprised and shocked by the gratuitous inhumanity of so many human beings, their spontaneous malevolence towards one another. There were on the boat three young civil servants, Millington and I going out to Ceylon, and a young man called Scafe who had just passed into the Indian Civil Service. There were also two or three Colombo business men, in particular a large flamboyant Mr. X who was employed in a big Colombo shop. It gradually became clear to us that Mr. X and his friends regarded us with *a priori* malignity because we were civil servants. It was my first experience of the class war and hatred between Europeans which in 1904 were a curious feature of British imperialism in the East.

The British were divided into four well-defined classes: civil servants, army officers, planters, and business men. There was in the last three classes an embryonic feeling against the first. The civil servant was socially in many ways top dog; he was highly paid, exercised considerable and widely distributed power, and with the Sinhalese and Tamils enjoyed much greater prestige than the other classes. The army officers had, of course, high social claims, as they have always and everywhere, but in Ceylon there were too few of them to be of social importance. In Kandy and the mountains, hundreds of British planters lived on their dreary tea estates and they enjoyed superficially complete social equality with the civil servants. They belonged to the same clubs, played tennis together, and occasionally intermarried. But there is no doubt that generally the social position and prospects of a civil servant were counted to be a good deal higher than those of a planter. The attitude of planters' wives with nubile daughters to potential sons-in-law left one in no doubt of this, for the marriage market is an infallible test of social values. The business men were on an altogether lower level. I suppose the higher executives, as they would now be called, the tycoons, if there were any in those days, in Colombo were members of the Colombo Club and moved in the "highest" society. But all in subordinate posts in banks and commercial firms were socially inferior. In the whole of my seven years in Ceylon I never had a meal with a business man, and when I was stationed in Kandy, every member of the Kandy Club, except one young man, a solicitor, was a civil servant, an army officer, or a planter—they were of course all white men.

White society in India and Ceylon, as you can see in Kipling's stories, was always suburban. In Calcutta and Simla, in Colombo and Nuwara Eliya, the social structure and relations between Europeans rested on the same kind of snobbery, pretentiousness, and false pretensions as they did in Putney or Peckham. No one can understand the aura of life for a young civil servant in Ceylon during the first decade of the twentieth century—or indeed the history of the British Empire—unless he realizes and allows for these facts. It is true that for only one year out of my seven in Ceylon was I personally subjected to the full impact of this social system, because except for my year in Kandy I was in outstations where there were few or no other white people, and there was therefore little or no society. Nevertheless the flavour or climate of one's life was enormously affected, even though one might not always be aware of it, both by this circumambient air of a tropical suburbia and by the complete social exclusion from our social suburbia of all Sinhalese and Tamils.

These facts are relevant to Mr. X's malevolence to me and my two fellow civil servants. None of us, I am sure, gave him the slightest excuse for hating us by putting on airs or side. We were new boys, much too insecure and callow to imagine that we were, as civil servants, superior to business men. Mr. X hated us simply because we were civil servants, and he suffered too, I think, from that inborn lamentable malignity which causes some people to find their pleasure in hurting and humiliating others. Mr. X was always unpleasant to us and one day succeeded during a kind of gymkhana by a piece of violent horseplay in putting Scafe and me in an ignominious position.

It is curious—and then again, if one remembers Freud, it is of course not so curious—that I should remember so vividly, after 56 years, the incident and the hurt and humiliation, the incident being so trivial and so too, on the face of it, the hurt and humiliation. One of the "turns" in the gymkhana was a pillow-fight between two men sitting on a parallel bar, the one who unseated the other being the winner. Mr. X was organizer and referee. Scafe and I were drawn against each other in the first round, and when we had got on to the bar and were just preparing for the fray, Mr. X walked up to us and with considerable roughness—we were completely at his mercy—whirled Scafe off the bar in one direction and me in the other. It was, no doubt, a joke, and the spectators, or some of them, laughed.

It was a joke, but then, of course, it was, deep down, particularly for the victims, "no joke". Freud with his usual lucidity unravels the nature of this kind of joke in Chapter III, "The Purposes of Jokes", of his remarkable book *Jokes and their Relation to the Unconscious*. "Since our individual childhood, and, similarly, since the childhood of human civilization, hostile impulses against our fellow men have been subject to the same restrictions, the same progressive repression, as our sexual urges." But the civilized joke *against* a person allows us to satisfy our hatred of and hostility against him just as the civilized dirty joke allows us to satisfy our repressed sexual urges. Freud continues:

> Since we have been obliged to renounce the expression of hostility by deeds—held back by the passionless third person, in whose interest it is that personal security shall be preserved—we have, just as in the case of sexual aggressiveness, developed a new technique of invective, which aims at enlisting this third person against our enemy. By making our enemy small, inferior, despicable or comic, we achieve in a roundabout way the enjoyment of overcoming him—to which the third person, who has made no efforts, bears witness by his laughter.

Civilization ensured that Mr. X renounced any expression of his innate, malevolent hostility to Scafe and me by undraped physical violence on a respectable P. & O. liner, but under the drapery of a joke he was able to make us "small, inferior, despicable, and comic" and so satisfy his malevolence and enjoy our humiliation to which the laughter of the audience bore witness. Even when I am

not the object of it, I have always felt this kind of spontaneous malignity, this pleasure in the gratuitous causing
of pain, to be profoundly depressing. I still remember
Mr. X, though we never spoke to each other on board
ship and I never saw him again after we disembarked at
Colombo.

Chapter Two

JAFFNA

W HEN we disembarked, Millington and I went to the
G.O.H., the Grand Oriental Hotel, which in those
days was indeed both grand and oriental, its verandahs
and great dining-room full of the hum and bustle of "passengers" perpetually arriving and departing in the ships
which you could see in the magnificent harbour only a
stonethrow from the hotel. In those days too, which
were before the days of the motor-car, Colombo was a
real Eastern city, swarming with human beings and flies,
the streets full of flitting rickshas and creaking bullock
carts, hot and heavy with the complicated smells of
men and beasts and dung and oil and food and fruit and
spice.

There was something extraordinarily real and at the
same time unreal in the sights and sounds and smells—
the whole impact of Colombo, the G.O.H., and Ceylon in
those first hours and days, and this curious mixture of
intense reality and unreality applied to all my seven years
in Ceylon. If one lives where one was born and bred, the
continuity of one's existence gives it and oneself and one's
environment, which of course includes human beings, a
subdued, flat, accepted reality. But if, as I did, one suddenly uproots oneself into a strange land and a strange life,
one feels as if one were acting in a play or living in a
dream. And plays and dreams have that curious mixture
of admitted unreality and the most intense and vivid
reality which, I now see in retrospect, formed the psycho-

logical background or climate of my whole life in Ceylon. For seven years, excited and yet slightly and cynically amused, I watched myself playing a part in an exciting play on a brightly coloured stage or dreaming a wonderfully vivid and exciting dream.

The crude exoticism of what was to be my life or my dream for the next few years was brought home to me by two trivial and absurd incidents in the next few hours after my arrival. It was a rule of the P. & O. not to take dogs on their boats and I therefore had to send out my dog, Charles, on a Bibby Line vessel. The day after my arrival I went down to the harbour to meet the Bibby boat. Charles, who had been overfed by the fond ship's butcher and was now inordinately fat, greeted me with wild delight. He tore about ecstatically as we walked along the great breakwater back to the G.O.H. and, when we got into the street opposite the hotel, he dashed up to a Sinhalese man standing on the pavement, turned round, and committed a nuisance against his clean white cloth as though it were a London lamp-post. No one, the man included, seemed to be much concerned by this, so Charles and I went on into the hotel and into the palm-court which was in the middle of the building, unroofed and open to the sky so that the ubiquitous scavengers of all Ceylon towns, the crows, flew about and perched overhead watching for any scrap of food which they might flop down upon. Charles lay down at my feet, but the heat and excitement of our reunion were too much for him, and he suddenly rose up and began to be violently sick. Three or four crows immediately flew down and surrounded him, eating the vomit as it came out of his mouth. Again no one seemed to be concerned and a waiter looked on impassively.

Millington and I went round to the Secretariat to report our arrival and we were received, first by the Principal Assistant, A. S. Pagden, and then by the Colonial Secretary, Ashmore. Ashmore had the reputation of being an unusually brilliant colonial civil servant and he gave us a short and cynical lecture upon the life and duties which lay before us. Then we were told what our first appointments were to be. I was to go as Cadet to Jaffna in the Northern Province. As I walked out of the Secretariat into the Colombo sun, which in the late morning hits one as if a burning hand were smacking one's face, the whole of my past life in London and Cambridge seemed suddenly to have vanished, to have faded away into unreality.

I spent a fortnight, which included Christmas, in Colombo and on January 1st or 2nd, 1905, now a Cadet in the Ceylon Civil Service on a salary of £300 a year, I set out for Jaffna with a Sinhalese servant, my dog, a wooden crate containing Voltaire, and an enormous tin-lined trunk containing clothes. In those days the journey, even without this impedimenta, was not an easy one. Jaffna, on the northern tip of Ceylon, is 149 miles from Colombo. To Anuradhapura, the most famous of the island's ruined cities, which was just about half-way to Jaffna, one went by train. From there northwards the line was under construction, the only section so far opened being the few miles from Jaffna to Elephant Pass through the peninsula. The only way to travel the hundred odd miles from Anuradhapura to Elephant Pass was to use what was called the mail coach. The mail coach was the pseudonym of an ordinary large bullock cart in which the mail bags lay on the floor and the passengers lay on the mail bags.

I had to spend the night at Anuradhapura, and I was asked to dinner by the Government Agent, C. T. D. Vigors, at the Residency. Here I had my first plunge into the social life of a Ceylon civil servant, a life in which I was to be immersed for over six years, but which always retained for me a tinge of theatrical unreality. There was Vigors, the Government Agent of the Province, an athletic, good-looking English gentleman and sportsman, a very genteel maternal Mrs. Vigors, and the tennis-playing, thoroughly good sort, belle of the civil service, Miss Vigors. Then there was the Office Assistant to the Government Agent and the Archaeological Commissioner, and there may have been also, but of this I am uncertain, the District Judge and the Police Magistrate. We were all civil servants. They were all very friendly and wanting to put the new boy at ease. The conversation never flagged, but its loadstone was shop, sport, or gossip, and, if anyone or anything turned it for a moment in some other direction, it soon veered back to its permanent centre of attraction. But we were all rather grand, a good deal grander than we could have been at home in London or Edinburgh, Brighton or Oban. We were grand because we were a ruling caste in a strange Asiatic country; I did not realize this at the time, though I felt something in the atmosphere which to me was slightly strange and disconcerting.

It was this element in the social atmosphere or climate which gave the touch of unreality and theatricality to our lives. In Cambridge or London we were undergraduates or dons or barristers or bankers; and we *were* what we were, we were not acting, not playing the part of a don or a barrister. But in Ceylon we were all always, subconsciously or consciously, playing a part, acting upon a stage. The stage, the scenery, the backcloth before which I began to gesticulate at the Vigors's dinner-table was imperialism. In so far as anything is important in the story of my years in Ceylon, imperialism and the imperialist aspect of my life have importance and will claim attention. In 1905 when I was eating the Vigors's dinner, under the guidance or goad of statesmen like Lord Palmerston, the Earl of Beaconsfield, Lord Salisbury, Mr. Chamberlain, and Mr. Cecil Rhodes, the British Empire was at its zenith of both glory and girth. I had entered Ceylon as an imperialist, one of the white rulers of our Asiatic Empire. The curious thing is that I was not really aware of this. The horrible urgency of politics after the 1914 war, which forced every intelligent person to be passionately interested in them, was unknown to my generation at Cambridge. Except for the Dreyfus case and one or two other questions, we were not deeply concerned with politics. That was why I could take a post in the Ceylon Civil Service without any thought about its political aspect. Travelling to Jaffna in January 1905, I was a very innocent, unconscious imperialist. What is perhaps interesting in my experience during the next six years is that I saw from the inside British imperialism at its apogee, and that I gradually became fully aware of its nature and problems.

After the Vigors's dinner, still an innocent imperialist, I returned to the Anuradhapura Rest House where I was to sleep the night and where I had left my dog, Charles, tied up and with instructions to my boy on no account to let him loose. He of course had untied him and Charles had immediately disappeared into the night in search of me. He was a most determined and intelligent creature, and not finding me in Anuradhapura, he decided, I suppose, that I had returned to Colombo en route back to London and his home. So he set off back again by the way we had come, down the railway line to Colombo. At any rate, two Church Missionary Society lady missionaries, Miss Beeching and Miss Case, who lived in Jaffna, returning by train from Colombo, in the early morning looking out of their carriage window at the last station before Anuradhapura and ten or fifteen miles from Anuradhapura, to their astonishment saw what was obviously a pukka English dog, trotting along wearily, but resolutely, down the line to Colombo. They got a porter to run after him, catch him, and bring him to their carriage. The result was that, as I sat dejectedly drinking my early tea on the Resthouse verandah, suddenly there appeared two English ladies leading Charles on a string.

The missionary ladies were aged about 26 or 27 and I was to see them again in Jaffna. Miss Beeching had a curious face rather like that of a good-looking male Red Indian; Miss Case was of the broad-beamed, good-humoured, freckled type. In their stiff white dresses and solar topis, leading my beloved Charles, frantic with excitement at seeing me again, on a string, they appeared to me to be two angels performing a miracle. I thanked them as warmly and devoutly as you would naturally thank two female angels who had just performed a private miracle for your benefit, and in the evening I went off with Charles and my boy to the "coach". It was only about two months since I had left London, grey, grim, grimy, dripping with rain and fog, with its hordes of hurrying blackcoated men and women, its stream of four-wheelers and omnibuses. I still vividly recall feeling again, what I had felt in Colombo, the strange sense of complete break with the past, the physical sense or awareness of the final forgetting of the Thames, Tilbury, London, Cambridge, St. Paul's, and Brighton, which came upon me as I walked along the bund of the great tank at Anuradhapura with Charles to the place where the coach started for Jaffna.

Over and over again in Ceylon my surroundings would suddenly remind me of that verse in Elton's poem:

> *I wonder if it seems to you,*
> *Luriana, Lurilee,*
> *That all the lives we ever lived and all the lives to be*
> *Are full of trees and changing leaves,*
> *Luriana, Lurilee.*

One of the charms of the island is its infinite variety. In the north, east, and south-east you get the flat, dry, hot low country with a very small rainfall which comes mainly in a month or so of the north-east monsoon. It is a land of silent, sinister scrub jungle, or of great stretches of sand broken occasionally by clumps of low blackish shrubs, the vast dry lagoons in which as you cross them under the blazing sun you continually see in the flickering distance the mirage of water, a great non-existent lake sometimes surrounded by non-existent coconut trees or palmyra palms. That is a country of sand and sun, an enormous blue sky stretching away unbroken to an immensely distant horizon. Many people dislike the arid sterility of this kind of Asiatic low country. But I lived in it for many years, indeed for most of my time in Ceylon, and it got into my heart and my bones, its austere beauty, its immobility and unchangeableness except for minute modulations of light and colour beneath the uncompromising sun, the silence, the emptiness, the melancholia, and so the purging of the passions by complete solitude. In this kind of country there are no trees and changing leaves, and, as far as my experience goes, there are no Luriana Lurilees.

But over a very large part of Ceylon the country is the exact opposite of the sandy austerity of Jaffna and Hambantota in which I spent nearly six years of my Ceylon life. It is, as in so many other places, mainly a question of rain. In the hills and mountains which form the centre of Ceylon and in the low country of the west and south-west the rainfall is large or very large and the climate tropical. In this zone lies Anuradhapura and nothing in the universe could be more unlike a London street than the bund of the tank in Anuradhapura. Everything shines and glitters in the fierce sunshine, the great sheet of water, the butterflies, the birds, the bodies of the people bathing in the water or beating their washing upon the stones, their brightly coloured cloths. Along the bund grow immense trees through which you can see from time to time the flitting of a brightly coloured bird, and everywhere all round the tank wherever you look are shrubs, flowers, bushes, and trees, tree after tree after tree. And for the next 36 hours in the bullock cart all the way up from Anuradhapura to Elephant Pass it was tree after tree after tree on both sides of the straight road. It was a world of trees and changing leaves, and all the lives of all the people who lived in that world were, above all, lives full of trees and changing leaves.

The only other passenger by the coach was a Sinhalese, the Jaffna District Engineer. It was a trying journey. The road from Anuradhapura to Elephant Pass had been cut absolutely straight through the kind of solid jungle which covered and still covers a large portion of Ceylon. If the bullock cart stopped at any time and you looked back

along the road as far as you could see and then forward
along the road as far as you could see, the road behind
and the road in front of you were absolutely identical, a
straight ribbon of white or grey between two walls of
green. In my last three years in Ceylon, I lived a great
deal in this kind of solid jungle country, for it covered
half of the Hambantota District where I was Assistant
Government Agent. It is oppressive and menacing, but I
got to like it very much. It is full of trees and changing
leaves, and therefore completely unlike the open scrub
jungle of the great treeless stretches of sand which in the
south you often find alternating with thick jungle. But
it is also quite different from the brilliant luxuriant foun-
tains of tree and shrub in which the villages lie in the
Kandyan hills and from the parklike luxuriance of places
like Anuradhapura.

Travelling through it by road, all you see is the two
unending solid walls of trees and undergrowth on either
side of you. The green walls are high enough to prevent
the slightest eddy of wind stirring the hot air. The jungle
is almost always completely silent. All the way up to
Elephant Pass I saw hardly any birds and no animals
except once or twice the large grey wanderu monkey
loping across the road or sitting in attitudes of profound-
est despair upon the treetops. Except in the few villages
through which we passed we met scarcely any human
beings. In the day the heat and dust were terrific; the
bullock cart creaked and groaned and rolled one about
from side to side until one's bones and muscles and
limbs creaked and groaned and ached. All you heard was
the constant thwack of the driver's stick on the bulls'
flanks and the maddening monotony of his shrill exhorta-
tions, the unchanging and unending ejaculations without

which apparently it is impossible in the East to get a bull to draw a cart. So slow was the progress and so uncomfortable the inside of the cart, that the District Engineer and my dog Charles and I walked a good deal, for we had little difficulty in keeping up with the bulls. But at night we lay on the postbags, the District Engineer on one side and I on the other with the dog between us. Each time that the rolling of the cart flung the D.E. towards my side and therefore on to Charles, there was a menacing growl and once or twice, I think, a not too gentle nip.

I left Anuradhapura at 9 o'clock in the evening of Tuesday, January 3rd, and the bullock cart with its broken and battered passengers arrived at Elephant Pass at 9 o'clock in the morning of Thursday, January 5th. The town of Jaffna, for which I was bound, was the capital and administrative centre of the Northern Province. It stood upon a peninsula—the Jaffna peninsula—which is connected with the mainland of Ceylon by a narrow causeway, Elephant Pass. As we approached Elephant Pass in the early morning, the country gradually changed. The thick jungle thinned out into scrub jungle and then into stretches of sand broken by patches of scrub. Then suddenly we came out upon the causeway. On each side of us was the sea and in front of us the peninsula, flat and sandy, with the gaunt dishevelled palmyra palms, which eternally dominate the Jaffna landscape, sticking up like immense crows in the distance. Everywhere was the calling and crying and screaming of the birds of the sea and the lagoons. It is an extraordinary change which never lost its surprise, the jet of exhilaration in one's body and mind when after hours in the close overhanging jungle one bursts out into a great open space, a great stretch of sky and a distant horizon, a dazzling world of sun and sea.

From Elephant Pass I took the train to Jaffna. The journey from Anuradhapura, 121½ miles, had taken me 40 hours, as I find from a letter which I wrote to Lytton Strachey on the day of my arrival. Today one does the journey easily in four hours. The difference is not unimportant. Up in one's brain and deep down in one's heart and one's belly, the quality of one's life is very much affected by its tempo; the tempo of living is itself enormously affected by the tempo of ordinary transport, the pace at which one normally travels from place to place. In describing my childhood I said that in those days of the eighties and nineties of the 19th century the rhythm of London traffic which one listened to as one fell asleep in one's nursery was the rhythm of horses' hooves clopclopping down London streets in broughams, hansom cabs, and four-wheelers, and the rhythm, the tempo got into one's blood and one's brain, so that in a sense I have never become entirely reconciled in London to the rhythm and tempo of the whizzing and rushing cars. And the tempo of living in 1886 was the tempo of the horses' hooves, much more leisurely than it is today when it has become the tempo of the whirring and whizzing wheels. But in Ceylon, in the jungle road between Anuradhapura and Elephant Pass, and again in my last three years in the south of the island, I had gone straight back to the life and transport of the most ancient pastoral civilizations, in which the rhythm of life hardly altered or quickened between the moment when some restless man made one of the first revolutions by inventing the wheel and yoking a bull to a cart and the moment when the restless European and his brand new industrial civilization began in the 18th century seriously to infiltrate into Asia.

I am glad that I had for some years, in what is called the prime of life, experience of the slow-pulsing life of this most ancient type of civilization. I lived inside it to some extent, at any rate in Hambantota, and felt a curious sympathy with the people, born and bred to its slowness, austerity, harshness, so that something of its rhythm and tempo, like that of the lagoons and the jungle, crept permanently into my heart and my bones. It was almost the last chance for anyone to see it or live in it. The railway was already undermining it in many places and, six years later when I left Ceylon, the motor-car had only just begun to appear, the instrument or engine which finally destroys the ancient rhythm and ways of primitive life. When, less than a year after I had jolted up the road from Anuradhapura to Jaffna in the bullock-coach, I went down to Colombo to take my exam in Tamil, Law, and Accounts, the railway had been completed and I travelled by train all the way to Colombo. As far as the great north road and its villages were concerned the tempo of transport and life had already changed from that of the bullock to that of the locomotive.

The train from Elephant Pass to Jaffna was slow, grunting, grinding. Though I was dazed by the bucketing of the interminable bullock cart and in a state of nervous trepidation and anticipation with regard to what awaited me in my first "station" at the end of the journey, I was fascinated by what I saw out of the railway carriage window. The Jaffna peninsula is unlike any other part of the island which I have seen (though it may be like parts of the Eastern Province which I never went to). It is inhabited by Tamils, who are Hindus and generally darker

and dourer than the Sinhalese. The Tamil crowd swarming on the station platforms or in the villages or in the
Jaffna streets has a look and air of its own, much less
animated (unless it is angry) and less gay than the Sinhalese in Colombo or Kandy or the Southern Province. I
lived for nearly three years in this purely Tamil district;
Tamil was the first eastern language which I had to learn
and I got to know the people fairly well. They have to
work hard and they do work extraordinarily hard to make
a living out of a stony, unsmiling, and not, I think, a very
fertile soil. I came to like them and their country, though
never as much as I like the lazy, smiling, well-mannered,
lovely Kandyans in their lovely mountain villages or the
infinite variety of types among the Low Country Sinhalese in their large, flourishing villages or the poverty
and starvation stricken villages in the jungle.

The Jaffna country is remarkable. It is covered with a
chequerboard of innumerable roads and I must have
bicycled over practically every one of them by the end of
my time there. But it is so dead flat that I never remember
having to ride up or down even a modest slope, let alone
a hill. It is thickly populated, and, as the Hindu likes to
live by himself to himself, every family lives in a house in a
compound which is surrounded by a tall cadjan fence. In
Jaffna itself and in the villages, the compounds are close
packed one against the other often for mile upon mile, so
that the road runs on and on between two long lines of
cadjan fences. Behind and often overhanging the fences
are tall trees so that you feel rather confined and con-
stricted in the hot, windless tunnel. The contrast is all the
more striking when every now and again you suddenly
come out of the airless heat of the villages into a stretch
of open country. Here again is one of those featureless

33

plains the beauty of which is only revealed fully to you
after you have lived with it long enough to become
absorbed into its melancholy solitude and immensity.
Everywhere the lone and level sands stretch far away,
interrupted only occasionally by a few black palmyra
palms. Out of the enormous sky all day long the white
incandescence of the sun beats down upon the earth;
towards evening it changes slowly to a flaming red or a
strange delicate mixture of pink and blue.

When I arrived in Jaffna, I was met by the Office
Assistant, Wilfrid Thomas Southorn, who eventually
became Sir W. T. Southorn, Governor of Gambia, and
who married my sister Bella. In order that the reader
may understand the autobiographical story of the following six years, I must say a few words about the organization of the Ceylon Civil Service in the year 1905. The
island was divided administratively into nine Provinces
and some of the Provinces were subdivided into Districts.
In charge of the Province was a Government Agent (always referred to as the G.A.), a senior civil servant of
20 years' service or more. The Provincial government
office or offices, the kachcheri, was always in the chief
town of the Province, and there the Government Agent
had his Residence. Districts were in the charge of an
Assistant Government Agent (the A.G.A.), a civil servant
of anything from six to twenty years' service. The A.G.A.
had his Residence and District kachcheri in the "out-
station", the chief town of his District; he was under the
orders of and directly responsible to the G.A., but, owing
to the long distances and difficulties of transport, he
usually had a good deal of independence and scope for
initiative. In 1905 the Northern Province was divided
into the Jaffna peninsula with the provincial kachcheri in

Jaffna town, and on the mainland two Districts, Mannar and Mullaitivu. The G.A. was John Penry Lewis, 50 years old; the A.G.A. Mannar was John Scott, aged 28, and the A.G.A. Mullaitivu R. A. G. Festing, aged 30.

In provincial kachcheris the G.A. always had two young civil servants immediately under him who did the office work, checking the accounts, issuing licences, going through all the letters, preparing the files and submitting all important questions for decision by the G.A. with perhaps a précis and, if they had any, their own suggestions or proposals. Of these two the senior was the O.A. (Office Assistant to the Government Agent) who might have anything from one to six years' service; the junior was called a Cadet, and every civil servant when he first arrived was attached to some provincial kachcheri as Cadet. It was in the post of O.A. and Cadet that the young civil servant learnt his job of imperialist administrator and to a great extent determined his future career. For your performance in the role of Office Assistant and your G.A.'s opinion of you had a considerable effect upon your career, for it influenced the minds of the great men far off in the Secretariat in Colombo, the Second Assistant Colonial Secretary, the Principal Assistant Colonial Secretary, and the Colonial Secretary himself, in whose hands rested your fate as regards promotion and appointments. Posts were either administrative, i.e. you were an Office Assistant, an Assistant Government Agent, or a Government Agent, or purely judicial, i.e. you were a Police Magistrate or a District Judge. Generally the administrative posts were considered to be a good deal more desirable than the judicial, and it was the young man who made his mark as O.A. who got rapid promotion to A.G.A. whereas the not so successful would probably find that he got a succession of judicial appointments. It must be admitted that success, in this sense, did not depend entirely upon your competence as a civil servant. A social analysis of the service in my time would, I think, have revealed the curious fact that, if you were thought to be not much of a "good fellow" or not much of a "gentleman", this was considered by the Colonial Secretary and his Assistants to qualify you for being a Magistrate or Judge rather than an A.G.A. (though this, of course, did not mean that no Police Magistrates or District Judges were good fellows or gentlemen).

Well, it was as Cadet attached to the Jaffna kachcheri that I arrived in Jaffna on January 5th, 1905. The station had a white population of ten or twelve government officers, perhaps ten missionaries, a retired civil servant with a daughter and two granddaughters, and an appalling ex-army officer with an appalling wife and an appalling son. For the purpose of accommodating myself to this society, of avoiding being condemned as not a good fellow or not a gentleman, I had some liabilities and three assets. One liability is the social defect which I have suffered from ever since I was a child, as I showed in the first volume of my autobiography, intelligence. Intelligence and the intellectual produced the same feeling of uneasiness, suspicion, and dislike among the white population of Jaffna and Ceylon as they had on the P. & O. *Syria*, in St. Paul's School, and in nearly all strata or pockets of English society. I explained in *Sowing* how in my childhood and youth I had developed, in part instinctively and in part consciously, a façade or carapace behind which I could conceal my most unpopular characteristics. The rather abortive wave of hostility on board the *Syria* against me and my fellow civil servants taught me the necessity of improving the façade and made me more fit to deal with Ceylon civil servants and planters. The process, I suppose, is what is popularly known as "making a man of him". It made, let us say, finally a man of me, though the man was and has remained three-quarters sham. What in fact happened was that I had put the finishing touches to a façade behind which I could conceal or camouflage my intellect and also hide from most people, both in Ceylon and for the remainder of my life, the fact that I am mentally, morally, and physically a coward. A particular liability was my 90 large volumes of Voltaire. Socially and psychologically they did me no good, and materially throughout my years in Ceylon caused considerable difficulty when I was moved from one station to another and they suddenly had to be transported over hundreds of miles in country which sometimes was without a railway. I am a little proud of the fact that socially I lived down the 90 volumes and physically brought them back to England in fair condition, neither repudiating Voltaire spiritually and socially nor abandoning him materially.

Of my assets the first, and perhaps least important, was three bright green flannel collars. I do not suppose that anyone now remembers that in 1904 a new kind of collar was suddenly put upon the market for men's clothes. They were of very bright colours, made of flannel, and you attached them by studs to whatever kind of shirt you chose to wear. They were, no doubt, a symptom of the moral breakdown of the Edwardian era, the revolt against Victorianism, particularly in so far as it affected the formal male respectability in dress with its boiled shirt and starched white collar. It is true that they went out as soon as they came in, and it may be that I was almost the only person who had the courage and bad taste to buy them. I know that Thoby Stephen, when he saw me wearing one, said: "My good fellow, you can't wear that sort of thing", and they were commented upon—as were my brown boots—most unfavourably by Lytton Strachey. In Ceylon for a short time they did me a great service. No one had ever seen anything like them before—or would again—and people were deceived into thinking that I must be a very up-to-date and dashing young fellow.

My second asset was my good dog Charles. I had bought him four or five years before from an advertisement in the *Exchange and Mart*, a paper which was of absorbing interest to us in my boyhood. In term time I used to take him with me to Cambridge, where he was more a liability than an asset, for I was not allowed to have him with me in my rooms in college. For some strange reason a wizened little Lord X—I have completely forgotten his name and hardly knew him at the time—kept him for me in his rooms in Jesus Lane. Charles was an extremely intelligent and affectionate dog, his one fault being that he was an inveterate fighter and hunter. It was, however, his faults which brought me fame and respect in Jaffna. On the very day of my arrival there he helped me to create a good impression, to develop my façade, and to do something to counteract Voltaire. The mere fact that I had brought a dog with me—which had hardly if ever been done by a civil servant before—was well thought of and began to counteract Voltaire, and the two things, the one so obviously right and the other so obviously wrong, helped to establish for me the privilege, which the most conventional Englishman is surprisingly ready to allow, of being slightly eccentric.

Charles immediately staged a spectacular act or rather acts which won us both approval. On my arrival in Jaffna I was taken in hand by Southorn, who introduced me to Dowbiggin, the Superintendent of Police, and Jimmy Bowes, the Assistant Superintendent of Police. The four of us, accompanied by Charles, walked into the vast ancient Portuguese Fort, where I was to live with Southorn in a bungalow upon one of the bastions. As we approached the steps leading to the great outer walls, a cat suddenly crossed our path and scrambled up and over a wall into a kind of dishevelled garden. In England Charles was well aware that he was not allowed to chase cats, but, I suppose, the imperialist Anglo-Indian spirit had already got hold of him and he thought that in any case a native cat was different. Ignoring my shout to him to come back, he was up and over the wall in a second, and from the tangle of shrubs rose a terrific din of snarls, growls, hisses, shrieks, and groans. Before I could get over the wall there was a sudden silence, and back over the wall came Charles, bloody and very much scratched about the face, but triumphantly carrying in his mouth a large, dead tabby cat. I saw that the dead cat and the rapidity of its murder had immediately given me, as well as Charles, considerable prestige in the eyes of Dowbiggin and Bowes, and even of Southorn.

But my triumphs and those of the blood-stained Charles were not yet finished. We went up on to the ramparts of the Fort and there Charles at once found among the weeds and bushes a very large snake. He seized it, luckily behind the head, and began to shake it violently as if it were a rat. It was a strange sight. With every shake he gave it, its body gave him a violent blow on the ribs and the tail curled round like the thong of a whip and hit him in the face on the opposite side of his body. The thuds on his ribs, the smacks of the tail on his face, and Charles's grumbling growls resounded regularly for some minutes and then the snake was as dead as the cat. My reputation as a good fellow, a Sahib, a man not to be trifled with, was therefore established within three hours of my arrival, for a civil servant, wearing bright green flannel collars and accompanied by a dog who within the space of ten minutes had killed a cat and a large snake, commanded immediate respect.

By a lucky chance I clinched the matter that same evening and again proved myself to be a man whom one cannot trifle with. My third asset was that I could play a competent game of tennis and a good game of bridge. Dowbiggin, now Sir Herbert Dowbiggin, was not at all meek and mild either in word or deed. He was a bad bridge player, but had bullied the other bad bridge players into accepting him as a good player and so had established himself as a kind of dictator of the Jaffna bridge table. Of all this I, of course, knew nothing that evening, when I was taken by Southorn to call on Mrs. Lewis, the Government Agent's wife, and found myself with her as my partner playing bridge against Dowbiggin and Southorn. In the third or fourth hand Dowbiggin revoked and, when the last card had been played, I claimed the revoke. He turned upon me, red in the face, and violently told me that I was talking nonsense. Emboldened by Charles, the dead cat, and the dead snake, I told him what cards had been played by whom and turned up the trick which proved that he had revoked. Silence fell upon the bridge table and I felt that something had happened. In fact what had happened, thanks to the green collar, the dead cat, and my ability to play bridge better than Sir

Herbert Dowbiggin (whom I got to like very much), was
that another dictator had fallen and I, rather like the hero
in a boys' school story, had "made good" my very first
day as a new boy. I was accepted as one of them by the
Sahibs of the Northern Province and therefore of Ceylon.

The company of white Sahibs of Jaffna and of Ceylon,
into which I now had to fit myself, formed a strange
society such as I had never known before and would
never know again. It was the product of British imperialism in Asia, and this kind of society, as imperialism
is dying out of the world, is itself vanishing, if indeed it
has not already vanished. A rather detailed picture of it
as it appeared to my bewildered and astonished eyes and
mind when I plunged into it in 1905 has a faint historical
as well as personal interest. At the top of it were the five
civil servants, the G.A., with his O.A. and Cadet, the
District Judge, and the Police Magistrate. The G.A. was
John Penry Lewis who had been in the service 27 years
and was now aged 50. He was a large, slow, fat, shy man
with one of those leathery or rubbery faces which even in
middle age, and still more in old age, remains the face of
a bewildered and slightly grumpy child, or even infant. He
was an intelligent man, but extremely lazy and not fond of
responsibility. This kind of inertia and habit of evading
definite decisions (particularly when it was really necessary
to decide) was, I think, common among civil servants in
the higher administrative posts. It was partly due, I suppose, to climate which tended to dry up and sap the vigour
of the older administrative civil servants who had inevitably spent a good deal of their lives travelling about
in very hot and unhealthy districts. Lewis really took
little interest in administration; he had the mind of an
antiquarian, a historian, or archaeologist. He was fond of

reading and of ferreting out curious facts about his Province. After I became his Office Assistant and he found that I liked responsibility and did not make mistakes, he left more and more work to me, and when he was promoted to Kandy and the Central Province, got me transferred there to be again his O.A. I was a year with him in Kandy where, I think, I did nine-tenths of his work; I know that usually I worked hard for ten or eleven hours a day. We never had much to say to each other, but I liked him very much and I think he liked me.

His wife, Mrs. Lewis, was the exact opposite of him. She was the kind of wife which so many slow, silent, shy men marry. Large, plump, floridly good-looking, she never stopped talking at the top of her voice. She exploited what, I think, must have been a thick streak of congenital vulgarity and went out of her way to say the most outrageous things at the most awkward moments. Lewis would say: "Really, my dear," deprecatingly, but with a chuckle, when she had reduced some unfortunate young man or woman to blushing misery, for her vulgarity amused him. She did not mean to make people miserable, but she had the mind of a mischievous, not a malicious, gamin. After a time I got on quite well with her and in some ways really liked her, tiresome though she was. She treated me with some caution, which, being so rare with her, I felt to be slightly complimentary (or perhaps uncomplimentary) to me. Listening to Mrs. Lewis— and I must have listened to her, silent myself, for an extraordinary number of hours in the years of our acquaintance in Jaffna and Kandy—I was again and again amused and indeed entranced to realize that she was a Jane Austen character complete in face, form, speech, mind—a Mrs. Jennings who had stepped straight out of

Sense and Sensibility, out of the Portman Square of 1813, into the Ceylon of 1905. I, like Elinor, desire to do "justice to Mrs. Lewis's kindness, though its effusions were often distressing, and sometimes almost ridiculous."

Mrs. Lewis, true to the type of all the Mrs. Jennings's who have lived since, and indeed before, 1813, was an inveterate matchmaker. In this character she once unsuccessfully tried her hand upon me, the other victim of her artless and embarrassing manoeuvres being a young woman friend of hers who came on a visit of several months to her. On the evening when Miss M's visit came to an end and she had left Jaffna (she lived in another British colony east of Ceylon), sitting on the tennis court after the game was over, I felt the strangeness of a few minutes' complete silence from Mrs. Lewis and found that she was observing me with a contemplative eye. She broke her silence by saying to me in a voice which echoed through the courts: "I hope you kissed Mary good-bye?" The question was meant to be, and was, awkward, for in 1905 kissing was much rarer, less public, and more significant than it is in 1960. This trivial episode gives, I think, a fair picture of how we lived and talked in the Jaffna of those days. Mrs. Lewis never again referred to Mary, and even later in Kandy, where the field for the matchmaker was far wider and more favourable, she never again tried to practise her art upon me. In all other ways she remained true to type as long as I knew her. A fragment of her conversation, which I find recorded by me in a letter to Lytton, shows her style: "Since writing the above I have called on the G.A. They are back from the Pearl Fishery now and I have had the inevitable dinner. Mrs. G.A. is the same as ever: her greeting to her husband when he comes into a roomful of people is: 'O Pen dear, you really are *too* fat, with your great ugly paunch sticking out before you.' "

The two other civil servants were the District Judge and the Police Magistrate. Sanders, the D.J., was a small, fat whisky-drinking man of 49 whom I never got to know well, because he was soon transferred to another station. Dutton, the P.M., was a strange character; a strange fate, partly due to me, befell him, but I will deal with him and his fate in greater detail later. This, as I have said, was the top stratum of Jaffna society whose social routine was incredibly regular. We all worked pretty hard during the day. When the office and the Courts closed and the Sahibs and their womenfolk feared no more the heat o' the sun, from our various bungalows we converged upon the node of the day and of society, the tennis court in the Fort. In the Ceylon of those days among the white people the evening tennis was a serious business, a ritual, almost a sacrament. Every evening regularly there assembled Mrs. Lewis, Sanders, Southorn, I, Dowbiggin, Bowes, and the two lady missionaries, Miss Case and Miss Beeching. Occasionally the Provincial Engineer, Waddell, would come, but it was significant that Dutton was never there. We played hard and seriously for an hour or more, though only Southorn was a really good and I a fairly good player.

When the light began to fade, we put on our sweaters, and, sitting in a circle, drank whisky and soda and talked. This was socially the peak of the Jaffna day, the ritual of British conversation which inevitably followed British exercise. It fascinated me and, in a curious way, I never got tired of its humdrum melancholy and monotony, for it revealed not only the characters of my companions, but the strange quality of our imperialist isolation. Besides the eight people mentioned above, who were players, there were non-players who came apparently for the conversation, sometimes the G.A. and nearly always a Captain X (I have forgotten his name), his wife and his son. Captain X belonged to a past age which seemed remote even fifty years ago. He had been an officer in the army, in a curious regiment of Malays, the Ceylon Rifles, which had been disbanded many years before. (Years later I got to know their descendants very well in the Malay village of Kirinda in the Hambantota District, for, when the regiment was disbanded, the Malay soldiers who did not want to be repatriated to Malaya—and there were quite a considerable number of them—were settled with their families in Kirinda, and had remained there intermarrying ever since). Captain X was a short, choleric, dictatorial, foul-mouthed old gentleman, almost a caricature of the stage caricature of the curry-eating Anglo-Indian colonel; regularly every evening he laid down the law for all of us, his loud strident voice monotonously revealing his contempt for "natives" and his irritation with young men like me. His mountainous wife sat nodding her silent and sinister approval. Of the son I can remember practically nothing.

In those days, of course, no "natives" were members of the Jaffna tennis club. Our society was exclusively white. The only Tamils admitted were the podyans, the small boys who picked up the tennis balls and handed them to us when we were serving, and the great Sinnatamby. I used to watch Sinnatamby with some interest, a big stoutish Tamil in a voluminous white cloth and towering maroon turban. He was the keeper of the courts and served us the drinks. He was extremely respectful, but I sometimes thought that I caught in his eye a gleam which belied the impassive face when some more than usually outrageous remark of the Captain or of Jimmy Bowes echoed up into the heavy scented immense emptiness of the tropical evening sky. He might have been a character in a Kipling story, and I could imagine generations of Sinnatambys standing respectfully behind their white masters in India right back to before the Mutiny—and some of them with that gleam in the eye getting their own back during the Mutiny.

The white people were also in many ways astonishingly like characters in a Kipling story. I could never make up my mind whether Kipling had moulded his characters accurately in the image of Anglo-Indian society or whether we were moulding our characters accurately in the image of a Kipling story. In the stories and in the conversations on the Jaffna tennis court (and off it) there was the same incongruous mixture of public school toughness, sentimentality, and melancholy. When in the tropics the glaring, flaring day ends with the suddenness to which the northerner never becomes insensitive and darkness creeps rapidly up the sky and over the earth, it is impossible not to feel the beauty, the emptiness, the profundity, the sadness in the warm, gently stirring insect humming air. Our talk after the game, as we sipped our whisky and sodas, consisted almost entirely of platitudes, chaff, or gossip, and yet it was permeated by an incongruous melancholy, which, if we had known the word, we might even have called Weltschmerz.

Like all Anglo-Indians and imperialists who were colonial government servants, we were, of course, "displaced persons". After two world wars and Hitler we all understand today the phenomenon and psychology of the displaced person. But that was not the case in 1905. Yet we ourselves on the Jaffna tennis court, though we did

not know the name, were in fact the phenomenon and had
the psychology of people whose lives had suddenly been
torn up by the roots, and, in a foreign country, had
therefore become unreal, artificial, temporary, and alien.
We all pretended to be tougher, more British, more home-
sick than we really were, yet there was a pinch of truth and
reality in all our posturings.

James Stewart Bowes, Assistant Superintendent of
Police in Jaffna, was an interesting example of all this.
His brother Freddy was in the civil service, highly intelligent, high up, and successful. Jimmy was the failure
of the family and had been found a job in the police. He
was 33, drank too much and whored too much, and was
already becoming fat and flabby. His only accomplish-
ment was that, like his brother, he spoke French like
a Frenchman—they had, I think, been brought up in
France. His language was of the foulest and his conversation generally lurid smut, but every now and again he
would break out into melancholy self-pity and sentimentality. In a letter to Lytton on February 27th, 1905, I
gave a description of him which is perhaps worth quoting:

I believe I have made the remark before but I can't
help repeating it, that the people in rotten novels are
astonishingly like life. All the English out here are
continually saying things of which, if you saw them in
a novel, you would say "people don't say those sort of
things". They are always sentimentally soliloquising
with an astounding pomposity. There is a horsey
superintendent of police here, very loud and vulgar and
goodnatured. He took me for a drive the other day in
what he calls his "English gig", and as we bowled
along under the palm trees he gave me the following

address interspersed with curses at the drivers of bullock carts who got in his way. "Ah, my dear Woolf, how I hate this bloody island. I shall have something to say to the Almighty when I meet him. I didn't ask for much, a little house in an English shire, with plenty of hunting and six or seven horses and enough money to run up to London for a week when the frost comes— Get out, you ugly stinking fucking son of a black buggered bitch; you black bugger you—I don't ask for much, I'd be as happy as a king—you greasy fat Jaffna harlot, get out of the light, you black swine— and I don't get it." It went on like this for a full half hour, and if you left out the curses and the language, you would find the same sort of stilted stuff in any of the swarms of 1st class books in the Union library.

I began my life as a civil servant in Jaffna by living with the O.A., Wilfrid Thomas Southorn, known to his friends as Tom Southorn. He was a year my senior. Jaffna was and is a biggish town. Europe has made a deep and wide impression upon the face of all the big towns of Ceylon which I know except upon Jaffna; in Colombo, Kandy, or Galle, the buildings, the private houses, the roads and gardens are Europeanized over quite a considerable area. But Jaffna, except in one or two conspicuous and dramatic places, is pure Tamil. It is what I think all large towns in Europe, and indeed the world, must have been before the 19th century, a swollen village or a congeries of villages which have coalesced into what we now call, because of its size, a town. After the 19th century in Europe and usually in Asia towns consist of a centre and a suburban area, and beyond the suburban area is "the country" and villages. The suburb is urban, as a rule horribly and hideously urban, and markedly different from the countryside and the rural village. When you pass from the town and its suburbs into the country you pass from one life or age into another. It is quite different in Jaffna; there as soon as you leave the main street, the esplanade, or the sea-shore, you are in a typical Tamil village of narrow roads between cadjan fences which hide whitewashed low huts or bungalows, bowered in trees. And the feeling that you are in an enormous village rather than in a town is the stronger because the population of Tamils is so thick on the ground in the Jaffna peninsula that in many places one village has joined up to another and to what is now the municipal area of Jaffna town. The consequence was that if I bicycled out of Jaffna to the opposite coast or to some far off village, as I so often did, even after a year or two when I knew the whole country well, it was extremely difficult to know when and where one had left the town and was in the country and a village.

These topographical details are not unimportant psychologically. They made the feeling of life in Jaffna quite different from anything that I have known else-where. And they increased, in a curious way, one's sense of imperialist isolation from the life of the surrounding country, even though at the time one was not really aware of this. For in the few places in the town upon which Europe had left its mark, the impression was dramatic and intense, and it was within these places for the most part that we Europeans worked and lived our lives. There were three such places and if you observed them with an historical and philosophic eye, you might see behind them the course of Ceylon history and the impact of Europeans upon it over three or four centuries. On the main street the Dutch have left their mark; it is half eastern and half Holland, many substantial houses, such as the Dutch built for themselves in Ceylon towns, with the characteristic stoeps. Down on the seashore it is a mixture of Holland and England in a number of houses solidly built, with porticoes and verandahs, in which lived white government servants, some wealthy Tamils, and an old retired Government Agent, Sir William Twynam.

But the third European enclave is the most impressive. It is a relic of the Portuguese occupation. The northern end of the main street opened into an immense esplanade or maidan, green with grass when the monsoons bring rain, but bare brown earth between the monsoons. There the Portuguese had built out of blocks of grey stone an enormous Fort commanding the sea. I suppose the area which it covers must be nearly equal to that of Trafalgar Square; it has a rather beautiful solidity and austerity; it is perfectly intact, the ramparts, walls, and bastions being exactly what they must have been when the Portuguese built them. It was characteristic of our rule in Ceylon that there was practically nowhere any sign of a military occupation. There was not a single soldier in Jaffna or in the Northern Province. The Fort had therefore been given over by us entirely to civilian use. The process must have begun with the Dutch for they built a church in it in the 18th century, and a Government House which in my time was only occupied when the Governor visited Jaffna. One side of the Fort had been converted into a prison and along another side a row of bungalows had been built in which lived the Superintendent of Police, the Assistant Superintendent of Police, and the District Judge. And perched up on one of the bastions was a bungalow for the Office Assistant.

It was in this bungalow on the bastion that I lived with Southorn. It was a rather gloomy house, overshadowed by an immense banyan tree which had covered the whole area between the verandah and the edge of the bastion with the tangle of roots and branches which is the sinister method of the banyan's growth. The tree was inhabited by a notorious and dangerous devil, so that the servants disliked the bungalow and would never go near the tree after dark. If you walked to the edge of the bastion and looked down upon the esplanade you saw below you a small erection which looked like a hen coop; in this there lived another devil or God whose power or reputation was considerable, for many people came to worship him. They sacrificed to him dozens of chickens by slicing their heads off with a sharp knife and you saw the headless bodies fluttering about on the ground. On grand occasions goats were sacrificed. At night great flocks of crows came and roosted in the banyan tree and all night through you could hear their melancholy rustling, cawing, and croaking.

The kachcheri was about a mile from our bungalow and every morning we used to bicycle to it down the long main street, Charles running by my side. The town was full of pariah dogs, usually lying about in the middle of the road. The first morning half-way down the main street three large yellow pariahs, each of them twice the size of Charles, flew at him. There was a terrific whirl of growls and snarls, of dogs and dust, and then after a minute or two three yellow dogs ran off into the adjoining compounds whimpering with their long tails between their legs. Charles had only a few superficial wounds. It is a curious fact that he was never again attacked in Jaffna; it was as if the news had been passed round canine society that it was safer to leave him alone, and as he was one of those fighters who never fight unless they are attacked or provoked, he lived the remainder of his short life in honourable peace.

The kachcheri is separated from the road by a small courtyard, and adjoining it at the back is the G.A.'s Residency. Both are solid grey buildings with broad verandahs and date, I think, from Dutch times. Attached to the Residency is what in England we would call a garden, but in Ceylon is called a compound. It was in fact almost a park,[1] with great trees planted so that they gave the whole place an air of beautiful stillness and, what was so rare in the blistering dry heat of Jaffna, of coolness even in the middle of the day. We sat all day in the office working, except for the hour we took off when we bicycled back to the bungalow for lunch or tiffin. I rather doubt whether any European ever really understands an important side of the East and of Asia, ever gets the feel of its castes and classes and individuals into his brain and his bones, unless he has sat hour after hour in a kachcheri, watching from his room the perpetual coming and going along the verandah of every kind and condition of human being, transacting with them the most trivial or the most important business, listening to their requests, their lies, their fears, their sorrows, their difficulties and disasters. There are many things in the manners and methods of a Sinhalese or Tamil who comes to a kachcheri to get a cart licence or to buy a piece of Crown land or to protect himself against a dishonest and malignant village headman or to ruin a hated neighbour which are exasperating and distasteful to a European, and many civil servants never really got over this initial annoyance

[1] I had forgotten when I wrote, that the Jaffna G.A.'s bungalow was actually called "The Park" not "The Residency".

and distrust. However much they liked their work and, up to a point, the people of Ceylon, as they walked into their office in the morning there was below the surface of their minds, when they passed through the crowd on the verandah, a feeling of irritation and contempt.

I too, like everyone else, was at first irritated and contemptuous. But gradually these feelings, when I was left by myself in the kachcheri to deal with the people and their business, began to evaporate and in the end, I think, they died out of me altogether. I liked unobserved to observe the perpetual procession of men coming and going on the verandah, to listen to their requests and enquire into their problems and complaints. We who live in the towns and urbanized villages of northern Europe have a social psychology radically different from that of the Tamils and the Sinhalese. Our ideas and feelings are limited, hard, distinct, brittle, a muted version of the ideas and feelings of the people whom we read about every morning in the *Daily Mail* or the *Daily Express*. Our instinct is normally to tell the truth, even if we don't know—as is normally the case—what the truth is. Our life is dominated by machinery, material as in the railways and social as in the intricate tangle of law and government. We live in a little walled box with a row of walled boxes on each side of us and another facing us. Our life runs between metal lines like the trains and the old-fashioned trams. It has normally nothing to do with the jungle where wild beasts like the leopard and the elephant roam or even the human jungle where the human beast roams. If we have a tree in our back garden, there is no devil, no Yakko in it. Of course, very deep down under the surface of the northern European the beliefs and desires and passions of primitive man still exist, ready to burst out with catastrophic violence if, under prolonged pressure, social controls and inhibitions give way. That is why, as I said before, if you get even a little way below the surface, you find that no one is an ordinary person. But normally the schoolmaster, the Sanitary Inspector, the clergyman, the daily paper, the pavements and lace curtains and police magistrates and High Court judges, the ego and the superego are far too strong for the id, and we may live our whole lives behind our lace curtains in the image, not of God or man, but of the rubber stamp and the machine.

The people on the verandah of the Jaffna and Hambantota kachcheris are, at any rate, not like that. I do not think that I sentimentalize or romanticize them. They are —or at least were in 1905—nearer than we are to primitive man and there are many nasty things about primitive man. It is not their primitiveness that really appeals to me. It is partly their earthiness, their strange mixture of tortuousness and directness, of cunning and stupidity, of cruelty and kindness. They live so close to the jungle (except in the Europeanized towns) that they retain something of the litheness and beauty of jungle animals. The Sinhalese especially tend to have subtle and supple minds. They do not conceal their individuality any more than their beggars conceal their appalling sores and ulcers and monstrous malformations. Lastly, when you get to know them, you find beneath the surface in almost everyone a profound melancholy and fatalism which I find beautiful and sympathetic—just as something like it permeates the scenery and characters of a Hardy novel. The result of these inconsistent and contradictory characteristics was to me extraordinarily fascinating, so that few things have ever given me greater pleasure than, when I had learned to speak Sinhalese, sitting under a tree in a village or on the bund of a village tank and discussing with the villagers their interminable problems, disputes, grievances. And when I revisited Ceylon for the first time, after fifty years, the moment when I felt fully and keenly again the life of the Sinhalese and the Tamils was when I found myself on the verandah of the kachcheris at Hambantota, Kandy, Vavuniya, and Jaffna.

During my first weeks in the Jaffna kachcheri I found the work intolerably dull and boring. The O.A. was responsible to the G.A. for all the work of the office, indeed administratively of the whole Province. All the correspondence passed through his hands and, if he was a first-rate civil servant, whatever was submitted for decision by him to the G.A. would be properly and clearly set out by him with a minute and probably a suggestion or recommendation. If the G.A. was travelling on circuit so that it might well be impossible to get in touch with him, as was often the case, the O.A. might himself have to make a highly important and difficult decision. One of the extraordinary things about the life of an administrative civil servant in those days was the variety of his work. The G.A. was responsible for everything connected with revenue and expenditure in his Province (other than expenditure on main roads, public works, and major irrigation works). He was at the head of the Customs, the prisons, the police. He was responsible for all municipal and local government, for all minor roads and minor irrigation works, for sale or development of Crown Lands, for welfare work, for law and order, and for a great deal of paternal government unknown in European countries for several hundred years. The machinery of his government was a large number of headmen, a village headman in each village and superior or chief headmen in charge of larger areas. Half his time was—or should have been—spent on circuit, in travelling round his Province acquainting himself with the characters and work of his headmen and the conditions of the people, considering possibilities of improvement and development, enquiring into requests and complaints, and settling the interminable disputes and feuds of village life. In these circumstances a vast amount of interesting and important work was open to the O.A., particularly if he was energetic and the G.A. a little lazy. The Cadet was in a very different position. Fresh out from England, completely ignorant, he was the maid of all work, the kitchen maid, the fag who had to learn his job by doing all the dull, mechanical, dirty work of the O.A. At the age of 24 I was an arrogant, conceited, and quick-tempered young man. My work in the office consisted of signing my name on licences and routine documents and letters, and of checking the accounts. After some weeks of this, my temper gave way and I told Southorn that I would not go on doing this, that I was just as good as he was, and that I must be given some of the interesting work. Southorn was an unusually good-tempered person; any other O.A. would have told me to go to hell, but he very weakly did what I demanded.

My letters to Lytton show that after that I got a great deal more than my due share of the extraordinary variety of work which a junior civil servant had to do in those days. Indeed within four months of my arrival in Ceylon and three months of my arrival in Jaffna, I was, to all intents and purposes, left for two weeks entirely and solely in charge of the Northern Province, because the G.A. was miles away and out of touch with Jaffna conducting the Pearl Fishery, and Southorn was trying to pass his examination in Colombo. For instance here is the description of an "enquiry" of a kind which G.A.'s and A.G.A.'s were continually holding, but which seemed very strange to someone who had only two or three months' experience as a civil servant:

April 9, 1905   10.30 P.M.

I am dead tired having bicycled about 35 miles. I had to inspect the stumps of some trees which had been cut down near a big temple. A violent dispute had arisen between two priests and one accused the other of cutting down trees on crown land. I had to decide whether it was crown land or not in the midst of a yelling mob of some hundreds of people. I must now go to bed, although I probably shall not sleep being perpetually kept awake by a big owl I possess. He is a wonderful bird: he looks hundreds of years old with the wisdom and malignancy of a fiend; the beauty and texture of his feathers is indescribable, the most astonishing mixture of greys and browns. All night long he chases a rat round the dog kennel in which I keep him, but as he never catches him and I never feed the rat, they are both slowly dying of starvation. It is questionable whether in the end either will have the strength to eat the other.

Almost the first thing I read in Tamil was this: "I saw a teacher and his disciple sitting under a tree; the age of the disciple was eighty, and the age of the teacher was eighteen."

In the end there was no tragedy to the owl. I took him one evening and let him loose and he flew away over the Fort and esplanade. He had been given to me by a police constable. I do not remember how I dealt with the rat.

Here is another letter to Lytton which recalls to me very vividly the atmosphere and savour of those early days in Jaffna:

May 21, 1905

A cataclysm is hourly expected here. Yesterday a headman came to the Kachcheri and reported that a hole had suddenly appeared in a field about 5 miles from Jaffna, that it was still increasing. I bicycled out to the place in the afternoon. It is in the middle of a perfectly flat plain and was the most astonishing sight I have ever seen. It is like a big pond with the water about a foot from the top, there is a curious heaving in the water, every five or ten minutes a crack appears in the earth round the edge, the crack widens and the earth topples over into the water which heaves and swirls and eddies. Hundreds of natives stand round, looking on with the usual appearance of complete indifference, and every time another foot of ground disappears, a long "aiyo, aiyo" goes up. The water is obviously from the sea which is about a mile and a half from the place and I expect it means that Jaffna Peninsula is going to return to the seabed from which it came. If the sea once begins coming in, there is absolutely nothing to stop it simply pouring over this huge flat plain which is never above and sometimes below sea level. If so, this is my last letter to you—and for dullness is probably only equalled by the first, which, I remember, went to France. But there is nothing to say to you, nothing to tell you of except "events". I neither read nor think nor—in the old way—feel. I can tell you that I rode 12 miles, after the usual work, to the northern coast to inspect a leaky ship, in which the Government is sending salt to Colombo: how I was rowed out in the moonlight side by side with the vast fat Chetty contractor who was responsible for the leaky ship: how I climbed about in the hot hold with the water pouring in, and examined the master and crew sitting on a campstool in a little reeking cabin: how I was rowed back through a little fleet of catamarans, fifty or sixty logs of wood bobbing on the sea each with a kneeling figure on it which outlined against the white sea looked like a ghost praying. I can't write about anything else; here are the only realities, and the curious feelings they excite, the only pleasant feelings. Perhaps they are not the only ones; when I read your letters first, you are for the moment real again. I can laugh too over Bob Trey—whose letter God damn it, I shall never answer—and every now and then you raise things even to the pitch of excitement. But for the rest it's either the curious feelings and excitement from these curious rare incidents and sights or else the boredom of work and the nausea of conversation.

The following is perhaps worth quoting as giving a picture of a Ceylon hospital in 1905:

Last week I had another study in sordidity which may amuse you—the Jaffna hospital. I happened to be with Dutton (who is really doing the magistrate's work) when he was summoned to the hospital to take the dying deposition of a man who had had his head cracked in a brawl. I walked over with him. The hospital consists of two long rooms bare and whitewashed, with rows of plank beds down each wall. Horrible looking dishes lay scattered about and on the planks lay three or four natives without any covering but the clothes in which they had arrived, their heads and bodies bandaged, groaning, grunting and spitting on the floor. Outside, and on the verandah and therefore to all intents and purposes in the room, squatted a crowd of patients and their friends talking, quarrelling, chewing betel and spitting it out upon the floor. Among these sat the dying man eating curry and rice out of a big dish, and quarrelling with the man who is accused of having broken his head. We could discover no attendant and so went off to ask the doctor what it all meant. All he could tell us was that he had given strict orders that the man should lie quite still doing nothing as he might fall down dead at any moment. The whole thing was exactly what I imagine the 18th century hospitals were like. . . .

By the by, have you read one of the supremest books, *Pilgrimage to Al-Madinah and Meccah* by Burton? There is no doubt we must go to Egypt and Arabia, and after all "Voyaging is Victory". Even here in this squalid little place, you have the curious absorbing people, and now and then there is a strangeness and beauty about a place that you never could have dreamt of in England.

Finally here is an extract from a letter of June 4th, 1905, which gives a glimpse of the work of a callow civil servant and of the mood of the moment:

I did not write to you last week, simply because I couldn't; and it was made worse by no letter from you.

After a year or two I don't think I shall write letters at
all. In a dim way, of course, I can realize what you are
doing, and how the hours go, but I don't see how it is
possible for you to imagine what actually I am doing
all day here. The worst of it is its futile fullness: one is
simply overwhelmed in the swamps of petty little
things. Pundits and work and tennis and law, it is
almost impossible to escape for a moment. They have
made me Additional Police Magistrate now: I spend
the evenings in trying to learn something about
the law; in the day the work is something of a horror
and a relief. At first it is a mere whirl: sitting in sheer
ignorance up there in the hum of the Court, writing
down the evidence, listening to the proctors and witnesses, thinking of questions to ask, trying to make up
your mind—all at the same time. I felt that at any
moment I might raise your old cry: "I resign". But it
is a relief after the dreary drudgery of the kachcheri.
Its sordidity is almost superb: you see all the curious
people and listen to their intimate lying tales. It is
impossible to feel that it is real, when I sit up there in
the stifling heat and look out over the glaring waste to
the Fort and the sea, and listen to an interminable
story of how one man smashed in the skull of another
with a stone because the latter asked him to repay a
debt of 25 cents. It is absolutely incredible how futile
life can be: and if one doesn't become engrossed in its
futility, I don't see that there is anything to stop one
going mad.

My letters to Lytton of this period are extremely
gloomy. Diaries and letters almost always give an exaggerated, one-sided picture of the writer's state of mind.

He is concerned to reproduce as vividly as possible—to make the reader feel as deeply as possible—a mood, only one of the many moods which chase one another all day and all night long through our minds and bodies. Even to ourselves we habitually exaggerate the splendours and miseries of our life and forget in the boredom of Wednesday the ecstasy of Tuesday—and vice versa. And when it is a letter that one is writing to an intimate friend of one's youth, the passions and prejudices of youth which were so important a part of that friendship exaggerate and distort the picture of our reactions to entirely new circumstances. This is certainly true of the letters which I wrote to Lytton in the early years of my time in Ceylon. I felt keenly the complete loss of the life which I had lived at Cambridge, its friends and friendship. In every conceivable way my life in Jaffna was the exact opposite. Intellectually I was back in school with the old sense of frustration. Much of the work was terribly boring. When I sat down to write to Lytton, all these feelings were so strong that they overwhelmed or eliminated all others. But even in these letters one sees between the lines interest, fascination, even cheerfulness breaking through.

In May, 1905, Southorn was moved from Jaffna and this had a considerable effect upon my life there for quite a long time. The Government sent to take his place as O.A. a man called Leak. Normally he would never have been appointed an O.A. for he was a senior civil servant. But he was extremely ill with T.B. and the Government sent him to the dry climate of Jaffna as the best place in the island for him. He was married and had a child so I had to move out of the O.A.'s bungalow and find a home elsewhere. This was by no means easy, as it was impossible to get an empty bungalow in a place like Jaffna and the only solution was to discover a government servant who had the room and was willing to take one in. Eventually I landed myself in the bungalow of the Police Magistrate, Dutton.

Dutton's character and career were odd and I propose to interrupt the narrative of my own life in order to pursue that of Dutton's in so far as I was able to observe it. Dutton was not a pukka Sahib and was not accepted as such by the pukka Sahibs of Jaffna. To begin with he was not a public school boy and had not been to a university. We were, of course, not all in so high a social category as that, but most of us could pass as "gentlemen". Dutton, in the opinion of Jaffna society, couldn't—his origins and his ways came too obviously from that depressing, dun-coloured, lace curtain region where the lower middle class merges into working class or vice versa. "A bloody unwashed Board School bugger, who doesn't know one end of a woman from the other", was the description of him given to me when I first came to Jaffna by Bowes or Dowbiggin, and it must be admitted that there was some truth in the portrait. He was a small, insignificant looking man, with hollow cheeks, a rather grubby yellow face, an apologetic moustache, and frightened or worried eyes behind strong spectacles. He always reminded me of Leonard Bast in *Howard's End*. He did not play tennis and he did not play bridge and did not mix at all in the white society of "the station", living alone in a largish bungalow with a piano, so it was said, and a vast number of books. The policemen, Dowbiggin and Bowes, hated him for being a lenient magistrate, and sitting on the tennis court after the evening's play I suffered hours of boredom listening to their abuse of him and of his decisions.

GROWING

For these reasons I hardly ever saw him during my first months in Jaffna. Now finding myself without a bungalow, I decided to ask Dutton to take me in. It was a bold step. I knew that the rest of Jaffna's white population would strongly disapprove, but I had built up a reputation of being an extremely competent civil servant and a somewhat formidable "good fellow" whose lapses from convention or good taste were condoned because, as they said, "of course, he's slightly mad"—how wrong they were!—so that I felt fairly secure that my career in the "Service" or in Jaffna society would not be jeopardized, as otherwise it well might have been, by my sharing a bungalow with "dirty Dutton". I therefore with some trepidation called upon him to ask him to take me in.

His bungalow appalled me. It was in a side street, smothered in trees, hot, stuffy, full of mosquitoes and geckos—not a breath of air ever found its way in. I found him sitting at a small table typing out incompetently on a decrepit typewriter the poetry which he had written the previous evening. Every evening Dutton wrote poetry, poetry incredibly feeble and of a sickly, sticky simplicity which, had I not read it—hundreds of lines of it—I should not have believed attainable by an adult in the 20th century. The vagaries of the human mind, the human heart, the human character in real life, so much more unbelievable than the most absurd creations of bad novelists, fill me with amazement. Who could possibly imagine that in 1905 an English civil servant, a Police Magistrate—what we now know to have been an imperialist—would sit hour after hour, day after day, writing poetry about fairies or, as he called them, fays? When not writing poetry, Dutton either read or played, with distressing incompetence, on a wheezy, out of tune piano.

Some of the notes of this piano had fallen in pieces and were now tied up with string, and he played on it for hours Gilbert and Sullivan, Mozart, the Gaiety and every other Girl, and impossibly sentimental German abominations.

The books which Dutton read surrounded him. There were hundreds of them, nearly all of them pocket editions and cheap series, like the Home University Library. They were ranged in bookcases which stood at right angles to the walls with narrow passages between them, and they and the piano filled the whole room except for a small space which housed a table, a typewriter, a chair, and Dutton. He was extremely nervous and suspicious and for some time the interview and the conversation were awkward, but eventually, when he found that I had read as many books as he had—or even more—and that I did not think poetry funny, he agreed to take me in, and I and my Voltaire joined Dutton and his Home University Library.

I have hardly ever known anyone so hopelessly incompetent as Dutton was to deal with life, and *a fortiori* with just that particular kind of life into which the cynical malevolence of fate had pitchforked him in Ceylon. The only possible way in which I can imagine he might have cheated fate or God or the Devil would have been for him to have obtained a safe, quiet post in the Inland Revenue or the Post Office and to have lived a life bounded on the one side by Somerset House or St. Martin's-le-Grand, and on the other by a devoted mother and a devoted old servant in Clapham or Kew. In Ceylon he lived the life of a minnow in a shoal of pike. The basis of his character was timidity which, as so often, was compensated underneath by boundless self-conceit. His lower class origin superimposed upon his timidity a deep inferiority complex which burst out in the most grotesque intellectual arrogance. He did not mix with his fellow civil servants and the other white inhabitants of Jaffna because he was afraid of them but also because, at the same time, he despised them. He must, I suppose, when a boy, have had a brain a good deal better than the average, and so he won scholarships which lifted him out of the welter of the elementary school into the Ceylon Civil Service. Unfortunately this meant that he was given the kind of education which completely addled his fairly good brain and destroyed every chance of his becoming a rational person. Literature, art, poetry, music, history, mathematics, science were pitchforked into his mind in chaotic incomprehensibility. When later on in Ceylon I became an extremely incompetent shooter of big game and, in cutting up the animals killed by me, saw the disgusting, semi-digested contents of their upper intestines, I was always reminded of the contents of Dutton's mind. As he not unnaturally disliked and temperamentally was frightened of the people and life which surrounded him, he very early escaped from them and it into books and the undigested, sticky mess of "culture" which they provided for him. His roots began and remained in Peckham, while his mind was full of Keats, the Gaiety Girl, Shakespeare, and fays—the result was lamentable.

In the months during which I lived with Dutton in his bungalow I got to know him extremely well, I came to pity him and with reservations to like him. Deep down under his muddled mind, his flinching and cringing soul, his crazy culture, he was a simple, nice person. My knowledge of books won his respect, and he very soon talked to me quite freely and relied upon my judgment in many things. For instance, he asked me to read the hun-

dreds of thousands of lines of his poetry and tell him what
I thought of them. This was a very ticklish business. His
poetry was, as I said, incredibly bad, and, when not about
fairies and similar poetical paraphernalia, was infected
with a curious kind of castrated eroticism. I suspect that
Dutton was physically impotent—and this accounts for
something in the events which followed; mentally he was
certainly a eunuch. He liked to talk about love and women
in a way which made me feel slightly sick. His attitude
towards them was a cross between that of a sentimental
and innocent schoolgirl and that of Don Quixote. He once
told me that sexual intercourse seemed to him repulsive,
and impossible with anyone with whom one was in love.
His naïvety in such matters was extraordinary and led
him into doing the oddest things, sometimes as Police
Magistrate in his Court. Here is an example.

Some time before I went to live with him, I was riding
home gently down the main street of Jaffna. I was
returning, I think, from tennis in the Fort. It was
evening, soft and sad with the long shadows falling across
the street after the fierce heat of the day. The houses had
built-out verandahs, screened from the road by great
rattan blinds. I was thinking of nothing in particular,
riding slowly, relaxed, a little melancholy. Being on a
horse I could see over the blinds on to the verandahs. As
I passed one of the houses, I happened to look into the
verandah and a Burgher girl sitting there smiled at me
and I smiled at her. A little further on I was crossing an
open space which led down to the seashore and my bungalow. Suddenly I heard a thin voice saying: "Sah! Sah!"
I looked down and there was a minute boy, about seven
years old, trotting along by the side of my horse. I asked
him what he wanted, and he said: "Sah! Sah! That young

girl ask whether she come to your bungalow tonight."
I very foolishly said yes, and she came and spent the
night with me. The "young girl", I discovered, though
the niece of one of my own very respectable clerks,
was a notorious Jaffna character—a "loose liver", as
they said; at the moment she was being kept by a Tamil
lawyer.

About three months after I went to live in Dutton's
bungalow, he told me one evening that he had had a most
unpleasant case to try that morning. The Tamil advocate
in question had brought a case against a young Burgher
girl for abuse and indecent language, alleging that she
had come to his house, where he lived respectably with
his wife and family, and in the middle of the day, standing in the street, shouted in a loud voice: "Come out,
you son of a whore! Come out, you son of a bitch!" and
had added details about the gentleman's life and prac-
tices which Dutton could not repeat. After hearing the
complainant, the accused, and their witnesses, Dutton
came to the conclusion that the woman was technically
guilty of abuse, but that morally she was a pure young
girl whose chastity had been unsuccessfully attacked by
the licentious advocate. This he said in Court, and, after
giving the advocate a moral lecture, he said that he re-
gretted having to convict a pure young girl of a technical
offence and to fine her ten rupees, and in order to show
his own view of the matter he would pay her fine himself.
So saying he took ten rupees out of his pocket and handed
them to the Clerk of the Court. As the pure young girl
was my clerk's niece and had, as I said, a notorious reputation in Jaffna, the whole incident and Dutton's little
speech gave the Jaffnese immense pleasure and amusement.

After I had lived some months with Dutton, I began to urge him to mix with other people and suggested that he should come with me one evening to the tennis courts. At first he refused, but I saw that he was rather anxious to do so, and that fear alone prevented him. Eventually he decided to come with me and play tennis, and so one evening, fitted out with tennis shoes and a racket, Dutton appeared, to the astonishment of the habitués, on the courts. Among the habitués or habituées were the two missionaries, Miss Case and Miss Beeching, who came to the courts solely, I think, because they wanted exercise. They obviously and with justification disapproved of the other habitués, including myself, and they very rarely stayed on the courts after play was over. They were bad players and usually played singles together, and I handed Dutton over to them; for the next few months Dutton used to come and play nearly every evening a hopelessly incompetent game of tennis with Miss Case and Miss Beeching. And I think I noticed, without really paying any attention to it, that sometimes the two missionaries would sit on after their game was over, talking in low voices to Dutton.

Then one Sunday I had to bicycle out to a place some ten miles from Jaffna to inspect a piece of land over which there was some dangerous village dispute. On the way back in the evening, to my astonishment I suddenly came upon Miss Beeching and Dutton, standing close together in a dry paddy field, each holding a bicycle and apparently engaged in earnest conversation. I can still see their minute figures, standing there in the gigantic, flat, dusty plain of the Jaffna peninsula, looking helpless, ridiculous, pathetic against the flaming sunset. And I realized that largely owing to me Dutton would marry Miss Beeching

—or perhaps it would be more accurate to say that Miss Beeching would marry Dutton. I like, as I have said before, the beauty, solitude, melancholy of great empty sandy plains, but just as when you see two human beings outlined against their flaming sunset, they contrive to make you see the human beings as two manikins, so too they tend to induce in me a feeling of impotence, the dwarfing and dooming of everything human in the enormous unpitying universe. I was depressed that Sunday bicycling back to Jaffna.

Some months later Miss Beeching did marry Dutton. Oddly enough, I cannot remember whether I was or was not at the wedding—I rather think I was not. At any rate, just about that time I was moved to another post, to Kandy hundreds of miles from Jaffna and for a long time I lost all sight of and touch with the Duttons. I saw them only twice again.

The first time must have been some four years later. I was now an extremely competent civil servant; my façade was in full working order. As a result I was Assistant Government Agent, Hambantota, having been given the post over the heads of many of my seniors, including Dutton. I worked sixteen hours a day, had chronic malaria and bad temper, and rarely saw a white man or woman. My fellow whites, when I did meet them, treated me as one of themselves, violent tempered and slightly mad, but on the whole what they called a good fellow. Dutton, despite Mrs. Dutton, had remained a failure in every direction; nothing could make him a good fellow, and so he was still a Police Magistrate, and in my last year in Hambantota I heard that he had been made P.M. of Matara, the district which adjoined mine on the way to Galle. As however I practically never left my District, there was no reason why I should ever meet the Duttons. But I did—twice.

The largest town in my District was not Hambantota, the headquarters where I lived, but Tangalla, thirty miles or so away. There was no railway and about once a month I drove or rode to Tangalla and stayed a night or two there in the Government Rest House. One evening on my arrival I found the Duttons in the Rest House; he had been ordered to come and try a case which, for some reason, the Tangalla Police Magistrate and District Judge—who was Southorn—could not take. The Duttons and I dined together, and after dinner we sat on the verandah with the Indian Ocean a few yards from our toes and talked. The conversation was curious, uneasy, and I felt—I could not say why—that every now and then it became tense and sinister. It was partly that the cosmic surroundings of the Tangalla Rest House once more, as upon the Jaffna plain, made the Duttons—and of course myself—appear to me minute, helpless, infinitely insignificant, almost tragically ridiculous. If I had to show anyone what God can do in the way of tropical nights, I think I should take him to the Rest House verandah at Tangalla. The small, insignificant building lies by itself in a small bay fringed with rocks and coconut palms. The ocean laps against the verandah. The evening air is warm and still and gentle. An enormous sky meets an enormous sea. The stars blaze in the sky and blaze in the sea. Every now and then—it seems almost at one's feet—a long, snake-like, black head rises out of the stars in the sea, remains for a moment motionless above the water looking at the stars in the sky, and then silently slides back into the sea. It seems incredibly mysterious, this black head emerging from the water to gaze at the stars in the sky, even though you know it to be only a turtle coming up to the surface to breathe. There is no sound in this melodrama of a tropical night except a faint lapping of the sea, and now and again a shivery stir of palm leaves. The sky, the sea, the stars, the turtles, the bay, the palms were so lusciously magnificent at Tangalla Rest House that Nature seemed to tremble on the verge—I don't think she ever actually fell over the verge—of vulgarity.

As the Duttons and I talked, we were embedded in, overwhelmed by this starry magnificence. Dutton and Miss Beeching had, I think, both changed. He seemed to have shrunk and she to have swollen. They reminded me of those pairs of insects—some are spiders or worms—in which a very small male is attached to a very large female—fitting ignominiously and neatly into her gigantic body—I sometimes think that this must be the ideal life for a male—and, after performing his male functions, is killed and eaten by her or just dies. Not that I thought that Mrs. Dutton would kill and eat Dutton; but she seemed somehow or other to have absorbed what little life and virility he had ever possessed. He spoke very little and sat silent with a vague, apologetic half smile on his face. She on the other hand talked incessantly. She had never liked me, had always disapproved of me, and I felt that her hostility remained. She did not, for instance, make any attempt to conceal her irritation at the fact that I had been given the Hambantota District while Dutton, who was five years my senior, was still only a Police Magistrate. Yet, as the evening wore on, the immense canopy of stars and sky seemed to overwhelm her and break down her reserve, even her hostility. I cannot now remember exactly what we talked about or what she said —it was principally, I think, reminiscences of the days in

Jaffna. But I was left with a feeling of tenseness, failure, and unhappiness. And in the feeble light of the oil lamp on the verandah I saw that the Red Indian face was puckered with worry and she looked as if she might at any moment burst into tears. I felt terribly sorry for them, but far more for her than for him. It became indeed so painful, this patter of expressed and unexpressed misery, that I made some excuse and went off to bed, promising to come and see them if I was ever in Matara. I never saw Dutton again.

But I did see Mrs. Dutton. Some months later I had to spend a few hours in Matara, and before paying my respects to the A.G.A. of the district I called upon the Duttons. He was away, but I found her at home in a two-storied house. She seemed to have grown even larger than before and was dressed completely in white in a voluminous, bride-like dress of some cambric kind of material. So voluminous was her dress that there emanated from her when she moved about the room the astringent smell of clean, new linen that one notices in large drapers' shops. The house was incredibly clean and shiny and smelt of soap and polish. I felt as if I had entered the hygienic aseptic ward of a hospital— so different from my bungalow with its immense shadowy grey rooms always smelling of books and dogs.

Mrs. Dutton had glossy black hair parted in the middle, worried brown eyes, and a complexion the colour of very pale copper. In her white dress she looked tragic and ominous. I felt extremely uncomfortable and wished I had not come. The conversation began calmly with the usual platitudinous gambits, but, as it went on, the feeling of agitation and tenseness which I had felt on the verandah of the Tangalla Rest House returned—also the continued sense of her hostility towards me. She was obviously in a

73

state of almost neurotic misery. And she began to express it, not openly, but obliquely, by continually returning to Dutton, his retiring nature, his failure in the civil service, the prejudice of everyone, including the authorities, against him. The more she said, the more nervous I became, and I began to get what was, I think, probably a delusion that she was accusing me of having been the cause of her marrying Dutton. As always happens when one is nervous, I became more than usually emphatic and sympathetic, and this made her still more agitated and unreserved. Suddenly overcome by panic, I said that I must go. She insisted that I must first see the house, and in terror I followed her upstairs and into their bedroom. Whether my nerves had given way and I was no longer seeing things as they really were, I do not know, but it seemed to me that I had never seen a bedroom like it. It was, like Mrs. Dutton herself, a mass of white cambric, the two beds being covered with the most voluminous white mosquito curtains I had ever seen. It looked as if the whole room was filled with bridal veils, and yet, perhaps owing to the overpowering smell of clean linen, it gave me the feeling of unmitigated chastity. It was the linen of nuns and convents rather than of brides and marriage beds. We stood one on each side of the beds and Mrs. Dutton broke down. I was so embarrassed and terrified that I cannot really remember exactly what she said, but she told me that her marriage was a complete failure, that Dutton was so queer that he ought not to have married, and that she was completely miserable, and, as she spoke, the tears ran down her cheeks. Keeping the beds between us and looking at her over the top of the immense mosquito curtains, I tried to calm her and eventually got her to stop her tears and come downstairs.

In fact, I persuaded her to walk with me to the Assistant Government Agent's bungalow. She would not come in with me, and as we said goodbye in the dusk outside the house, I ventured nervously to pat her on the shoulder. I never saw Mrs. Dutton again, and a year or two later, when I had left Ceylon for good, I heard in England that Dutton had died of tuberculosis.

To return to my own life in Jaffna, it was varied and pretty strenuous. Leak was too ill to do any work and so I had to do the work of both the O.A. and the Cadet. I also sometimes had to act as Superintendent of Police. In a letter to Lytton I tell him of an incident which shows the kind of thing one had to do as a Superintendent of Police. A Police Constable came to my bungalow early in the morning and told me that a small boy had disappeared and that it was thought that he had been taken away by a young man in a bullock cart to the coast at Kangesanturai, 15 to 20 miles away. The parents were in a desperate state, thinking that he might have been murdered, and they had set off for Kangesanturai. I too set off for the same place immediately on my bicycle, accompanied by a Police Sergeant. Some distance from Kangesanturai a policeman was waiting on the road to stop us and take us to the Chief Headman's, the Maniagar's house. There we found a young man and a crowd of relations of the small boy, together with headmen and the policeman.

The story was this: the child had been last seen with a young man in a bullock cart driving towards the coast. The young man was known to keep a dancing girl and therefore to be habitually in debt. The child's relations, when they heard this, set off in a body on the main road to the sea, stopping every bullock cart they met and searching it. At 2 in the morning they met a cart with the young man in it; they dragged him out, searched him, and found the boy's jewellery on him. Then they took him to the Maniagar's house, beat him with sticks and whips, pushed pins down his nails, and tortured him generally until he confessed. He said that he had taken the boy to Kangesanturai, carried him out into the sea, knelt on him in the water until he was drowned, took his gold ornaments, and then threw the body out into the sea. I set off at once to the sea, accompanied by police, headmen, the accused, and the child's relations. The young man took us to the place where he had thrown the body into the sea. The headmen collected 20 or 30 villagers and all day long we toiled over the burning blinding white sand watching the men wading along the shore searching for the body. We did not find the body. I knew there was a ship lying off Jaffna, the *Serendib*—it was the Government's Pearl Fishery boat—and I sent a note to the captain, telling him what had happened and asking him whether he could help us in the search for the body. Some days later I received the following characteristic letter from him—I found it among my papers, I don't know why I should have kept it for 55 years. It is perhaps not surprising that the Master of the *Serendib*, who spent his time coasting round the north of Ceylon, is a year out in the date of his letter:

S.S. *Serendib*
> Kangesanturai
>> June 18th, 1904

Asst. Supt. Police
    Sir,
    I received your note this morning and came on here immediately to see you but you had gone to Jaffna.
    I found it was not possible for me to get under weigh

again today as it is blowing very hard to the westward with a rough sea and I think it be a fruitless search besides my coals are running short and have just enough to carry me to Pamban and should I have gone out today I should have had to come back from Delft to Kayts to get some more.

I leave here for Delft at six tomorrow morning and shall keep a good look out on the way.

I don't think the body will have gone seaward yet as it has not had time to float and the way the tides set it will be found on the beach if found at all.

                    Yours most
                    respectfully
                    J. H. Rhodes
                    Master

P.S. We give a drowned man from 7 to 9 days to float but he must have weighed the child down.

Send the prisoner on board here and I will take him out tomorrow morning with a firebar round his neck and I'll drop him in 9 fathoms.

This letter is written in very fine copperplate handwriting. I do not remember whether the boy's body was ever found or whether the accused was hanged. The headmen's and police methods of dealing with accused people horrified me. In those days, as I soon learned, it was a perpetual—and usually losing—struggle to prevent every kind of pressure, including physical violence and torture, being applied to the accused in order to extract a confession. But if the treatment of the criminal was savage, the treatment of his victim was not much better. In another letter about the same time I described how I had taken the deposition of a dying man:

77

I rode to a place called Pt. Pedro on Sat. afternoon, partly on business, partly in order to escape Jaffna. It is about 21 miles away. I thought I should come back by a mad way and started out down the coast where there were no roads only sand and palmyra trees. No one ever goes there and the sand has heaped itself up into great curves and ridges. It seemed to be absolutely uninhabited except for one enormous temple standing quite solitary in this wilderness of sand. At last the track I had been following disappeared altogether and I had to haul my bicycle across a dried up lagoon in the direction I imagined my road to lie. Eventually I found myself at a Rest House 12 miles from Jaffna: there I inspected the tracing of a new road and pushed my bicycle through two miles of paddy fields. I got back at 7, scorched, aching, and sore, only to be met by a constable with a letter asking me to take a dying deposition of a man who had been stabbed in a fight. Only a Magistrate can do this so off I dragged myself to the hospital. It is fairly grim; the man was a mass of wounds, he lay on a bare wooden bed in the long gloomy room surrounded by all the other loathsome patients. It took an hour and a half to get his story out of him and it had to be interrupted by the man having to have his urine drawn, a filthy operation. In the end he became unconscious or pretended to be. It must be pleasant to be in a dying condition and be shouted at until you are forced to tell who stabbed you. I shall write an article (strictly anonymous) on Modern Humanitarianism in the East for the *Independent*. I wonder if things are really managed in England as they are here.

At the time I wrote this, I was too inexperienced to be

able to take a line of my own. Later when I had found my feet and knew all the snags as well as the ropes, I did what I could. But I was never a full-time Police Magistrate and only acted occasionally as Superintendent of Police, and one soon found, as I said above, that it was extremely difficult to prevent effectively the primitive and illegal methods of the police and headmen in dealing with crime. I am all and always upon the side of law and order, and my time in Ceylon, where I was on the Government side of the fence, strengthened me in this attitude, simply because without law and order, strictly enforced, life for everyone must become poor, nasty, brutish, and short. And the nearer one gets to the criminal, the more closely one has to deal with him, as one does when one is on the Government side of the fence in the administration or on the Bench or in the police, the less sentimental sympathy one gets for him, for he is usually a very nasty and brutish man. But in my case, actual experience from the inside of the administration of law and of what is called justice produced in me an ineradicable and melancholy disillusionment with those whose duty it is to do justice and protect law and order. Too often one watches the line between the criminal and the policeman or the judge growing thinner and thinner. As I pointed out in *Sowing*, the faces of eminent judges of the High Court of Justice suggest that nastiness and brutishness are found upon the Bench as well as in the Dock.

Towards the end of my first year in Jaffna, in 1905, I was again in difficulties over a house to live in. I had to move out of Dutton's bungalow, I suppose because he was to get married, and I could find nowhere to go. At last a Government Surveyor called Shipton offered to take me in for a week or so, but the first day I moved in a catastrophe

befell me which for the time solved my housing problem.
I got typhoid. I know exactly how I got it. In the
north-west shoulder of the mainland across the sea from
Jaffna there had been a complete failure of rain and
a minor famine had fallen upon the unfortunate inhabitants. We started a relief work at Punakari, the building
of a road. The people worked on the road and were paid
in rice and every fortnight I sailed across to superintend
the work and see that the people received their rice. It was
a pretty strenuous operation. I sailed in an open Tamil
boat with no protection from the sun and, as the bottom
of the boat was usually full of the most ancient and
fish-like smelling bilge water, the sun and stench combined
were formidable. Punakari was one of the most desolate and out of the way places in Ceylon. There was
no road to it from anywhere and that was why I had to
get to it by boat. It was an extraordinary desert of
sand; thick jungle began four miles from the sea, and
between the sand and the jungle stretched a large area
of dry, parched paddy fields. In the middle was a small
ancient Dutch fort, converted into a Rest House in which
I stayed. For several hours I trudged about in the blazing
sun inspecting what was being done and the number of
workers, and calculating how much rice would be needed
for next week. Then I sailed back to Jaffna.

I had to do this every two weeks, and on my return
from the third or fourth visit the wind suddenly dropped
completely and we lay becalmed.

All in a hot and copper sky
The bloody Sun, at noon,
Right up above the mast did stand,
No bigger than the Moon.

JAFFNA

Hour after hour, hour after hour,
We stuck, nor breath nor motion,
As idle as a painted ship
Upon a painted ocean.

"A weary time! a weary time!" just as the ancient mariner found it. The sun and the glare of the sun upon the sea were intolerable. The bilge was fouler even than usual, the stench more nauseating; flies swarmed over the boat, the bilge, one's hands and face. I had brought some food with me and managed with difficulty to eat a little of it. It would have been much better if I had not, for there is no doubt that the bilge, the food, and the flies combined to give me typhoid.

The afternoon I moved into Shipton's bungalow I had a bad headache and next morning I woke up feeling wretched. I hardly knew Shipton and I did not like to tell him that I felt ill, so I crawled out of bed and joined him at breakfast on the verandah. There is an eastern dish called hoppers, which is I believe a corruption of the Tamil "appam"; it is a kind of thick rice pancake which many Europeans in my time liked very much. Even at the best of times, when I was not suffering from typhoid fever, I was not very fond of them. That morning when the good Shipton put before me a plate on which sat two hoppers and on each rather greasy hopper sat a rather greasy fried egg, I felt as if my last moment had come. Shipton saw my difficulty and I had to confess that I felt extremely ill. He took my temperature which was very high. He must have been an unusually sensible man, for he did not assume, as nearly everyone else in Jaffna would have assumed, that I had malaria. He decided that I must see a doctor, but the difficulty was that there was no good doctor and no hos-

pital in Jaffna which could take a European. He then took
a step which almost certainly saved my life. About 6 or
8 miles from Jaffna there was a village called Manippay
in which was an American mission with a small hospital
and an American doctor in charge. Shipton went off to
Manippay and brought the American doctor to see me.
He immediately diagnosed typhoid and agreed to take me
into his hospital. I was put on to a mattress, carried out
and put into a bullock cart, and driven away to Manippay.
There we were confronted with difficulties, though I was
in no state to realize them. There was nowhere in the
hospital itself any place suitable for a sick European. I
had therefore to be placed in a small, completely bare out-
house which had only one small window about ten foot
from the floor.

The doctor, who was an extraordinarily nice man, told
me that I had typhoid, and that if I laid absolutely as still
as possible and ate practically nothing, my temperature,
which was over 103, would gradually go down and precisely on the twenty-first day would be normal, 98·4, and I
should have recovered. The hospital was terribly under-
staffed; he had only one trained nurse, a Tamil girl, who
had never touched a white patient and would probably be
too shy to do so. This proved to be the case; she came
occasionally into the room, but always stood a long way
from the bed so that she could not even put the ther-
mometer into my mouth. In the end I always took and
recorded my temperature on the chart and it was my
Tamil servant Appukutty who nursed me patiently and
efficiently for the three weeks. It was a strange three weeks.
I lived in a kind of twilight world, physically and mentally. They gave me nothing to eat except from time to
time a cup of Benger's food, I think it was called. I have

always had an infinite capacity of sleeping when I want to sleep and I slept almost the whole three weeks away. Somewhere, too, deep down in me I had an iron determination not to die. One day after I had been there a week or ten days, I woke to find three white-robed, turbaned headmen standing by my bed. They salaamed and one of them stepped forward and said: "Sir, we heard that you are ill and dying, so we have come to pay our respects to you." For a moment I thought it was a dream, but when I realized its reality, I was so much amused by the words and the solemn spectacle that I felt that the crisis was past and that I should certainly recover. And so it was, for punctually on the twenty-first day, when I took my temperature, it was for the first time normal.

I suppose it must have been another ten days or a fortnight before I was allowed to leave the hospital. Since childhood I have rarely had an illness severe enough to be followed by what one can accurately call convalescence. But when I have, the misery and horrors of convalescence have always seemed to me infinitely worse than those of the illness. Typhoid seemed to have drained all strength out of both body and brain. Someone—I forget who— took me for a few days into his bungalow down on the shore of the Jaffna lagoon and one evening I foolishly crawled along the road to the Fort and sat watching the tennis. On my way back suddenly I felt as if my last hour had come; my heart began to beat as if I had an electric drill inside me and the sky turned black while the earth began revolving round me. I sat down by the side of the road and eventually crawled home to bed. Then I got three weeks' leave and went off first to Kandy and then to Bandarawela. Here I stayed in a hotel up in the mountains. It has a most delicious and exhilarating climate.

When I first got there, I could miserably totter along for a quarter of a mile; a week later I had completely recovered and could walk five or ten miles and enjoy it. The following extracts from letters which I wrote to Lytton from Bandarawela in January, 1906, recall the place and my mood in it:

I was four days in Kandy and three in Hatton, an immense empty hotel surrounded by an interminable series of tea-covered hills, and now I have practically settled down for two weeks here. You can't understand my mood—and I don't think I can give its tone to you at all—without an idea of this country. It has enmeshed me together with my appalling isolation. It is superb; don't you think it always is when you can see vast distances? Well, here wherever you walk you can see over enormous tracts, but instead of, as usually happens in these cases, seeing plains, it is one immense sea of hills. You stand upon one and they rise and fall all round you in great waves, not rugged but desolate, covered with coarse grass, almost bare of trees. It is only to the east that there is anything dark and rugged where they rise up 2500 feet above this place in a long dark chain covered with jungle. The air is wonderfully soft and clear and the sky a curiously pale blue. I walk out on to these and wander about from 7–9 every morning and 4–6 every evening, the rest of the day I read Voltaire's letters, Huysmans, and Henry James. The only people I talk to are a man who drives a traction engine and an interminable procession of tea-planters. The latter are typically "good fellows": they ask me to come and stay with them and I accept and then put it off in terror. Somehow or other though I

can talk to them there is a horrible feeling of boredom
and awkwardness. One must always say the same
things in the same cheery way, and, as I do of course,
the awkwardness is only felt by myself. I have definitely
promised to stay next week with two of them on their
estates about 10 miles away: I shall have to but I dread
it. . . . An American whom I met at Hatton gave me
the following recipe for happily spending one's days:
"Take a quiet walk, have your meals, clean your boots,
take out your clothes and see that they are all right,
read and answer your letters, talk to anyone you come
across, go to bed", and "fuck your wife" I added and
enraged him.

. . . I stayed with the planters some days and, of
course, it was much better than I expected. One was a
wild maniac of the kind I am always surprised at being
able to get on with, typically, this is a repetition, an
ordinary very good fellow. The other was curious: he
had been at Selwyn destined for the church. He had
never thought until he began to read theology and that
reduced him immediately to agnosticism. Then he
became a private tutor, and tried to reform the method
of teaching, his object being to teach people to think.
He is rather charming and strenuous and deals
largely in philosophy. We had, before an admiring
audience on whom he has completely impressed himself, a violent argument about the existence of time and
he is now about to begin a study of *Principia Ethica*.
One would hardly expect an evening like I had in an
isolated hill bungalow on a Ceylon tea estate.

These extracts are from letters written on January 13th
and 28th, 1906. On January 28th I received a telegram

from the G.A. Jaffna asking me whether I was well enough to take up in the middle of February a special appointment as Koddu Superintendent at the Pearl Fishery. It was obviously an extremely interesting job, so I wired back "Yes", and next day set out to Jaffna.

The Ceylon Pearl Fishery is said to go back to very ancient times. The pearl oyster (Pinctada), which is more nearly related to the mussel than to the edible oyster, breeds on the pearl banks in the Gulf of Mannar some miles off the barren uninhabited coast of the Mannar District in the Northern Province. The oysters breed and produce pearls very erratically. In my day there was a Superintendent of Pearl Fisheries, Hornell, who had a steamer at his disposal and, I think, a dredger. He inspected the oyster banks in the autumn and if he found that there were sufficient mature oysters and the average number of pearls in the samples dredged up was satisfactory, the Government proclaimed a Pearl Fishery for the following February. As the Fishery was in the Northern Province waters, the G.A. Jaffna was in complete charge of it and had to make all the arrangements for it. He took with him four or five white officers. In 1906 he had three civil servants, John Scott, the A.G.A. Mannar, and two specially seconded, i.e. Malcolm Stevenson (three years my senior) and myself, and an Assistant Superintendent of Police.

The Pearl Fishery camp was always at Marichchukaddi, which as the crow flies is about 80 miles from Jaffna. When there is no Fishery, Marichchukaddi is merely a name on a map, a stretch of sandy scrub jungle with the thick jungle beginning half a mile or so inland. There was no road to it, only a rough sandy track along the coast to Mannar, so that the only way to reach it was by sea.

JAFFNA

There was no harbour and all the bigger boats and steamers from India and Colombo had to lie anchored offshore. About twenty to thirty thousand people came from all over Asia to the Fishery, divers, jewellers, dealers, merchants, traders, financiers, shopkeepers, dacoits, criminals. To house these people the Government, i.e. the G.A., built a large town on the desert of sand, containing bungalows for himself and the other Government officers, huts for the divers, traders, and boutique keepers, a court, police station, prison, and hospital. All these buildings were of timber with cadjan roofs. This temporary town was laid out in regular streets: Main Street, Tank Street, New Street, New Moor Street.

It was, I think, on February 15th that I sailed from Jaffna to Marichchukaddi in an open native boat. It took me a day and a half to reach Marichchukaddi. I lay on a mattress with the sun beating down upon me during the day and the immense canopy of stars seemingly just above my head at night. We had to sail first south-west round Mannar and through the little islands of Adam's Bridge and then south to the Fishery. There is—or was—to me always something extraordinarily romantic in this kind of setting off entirely alone in a small boat into the unknown. The wind would fall and we lay becalmed in an immense silence and then the breeze would again steal up across the water and we would begin once more to go gently through the sea. It really was as though time stood still. One's life, one's universe had been reduced to the bare sea and the bare sky, day and night, sun and stars. Whether or when one was to arrive lost all importance; the complete solitude away from any trace of civilization or taint of civilized people, with its gentle, soothing melancholy, seemed, as it always does, to purge the passions. When they ran my boat up on to the sandy beach at Marichchukaddi and I jumped down into the sand, I felt that, though my body was unwashed and unshaved, my mind had been curiously cleaned and purified. Naturally I was instantly and appropriately recalled to reality. The G.A.'s bungalow had been built on a small hillock of sand overlooking the beach and I walked up the slope to report my arrival and find out where my bungalow would be. When I reached the top, there was Mrs. Lewis sitting outside the bungalow with a table by her side and a gramophone on the table blaring into the evening sky above and the sand and sea below "Funiculi, funicula". "Hallo! Hallo! Mr. Woolf. I'm glad to see you", the jolly female voice was louder even than the Neapolitan singers. "How are you? Come on, come on and have a drink and listen to my new record." I was back once more in civilization.

It was certainly a very primitive form of civilization, apart from Mrs. Lewis and her gramophone. The methods on which we ran the Fishery seemed to me antediluvian, primordial. The fishing was actually done by Arab or Tamil divers. There were 4,090 Arabs who came down from the Persian Gulf in dhows. The dhows were commanded by chiefs or sheiks, some of whom, I think, commanded several dhows. There were 4,577 Tamil and Moor divers, most of whom came from India; they fished from open native boats. The Fishery lasted from February 20th to April 3rd. Every morning about 2 or 3 a.m., if the wind and sea were favourable, the Superintendent fired a gun which was the signal that the dhows and boats might be launched and sail off to the Pearl Banks. The method of fishing was this: each diver (if he was an Arab, using a bone nose-clip) stood on a large flat stone through which ran a rope held by a man in the boat, called a man-duck. At a signal from the diver the man paid out the rope as fast as he could and the diver on the stone was carried to the floor of the sea. There he shovelled oysters into a large basket which was attached to another rope. When he shook the rope, he was hauled up by his man-duck into the boat. This went on all day. There were 473 boats divided into two fleets which fished on alternate days; the largest number of boats to go out on any one day was 286. In the afternoon the Superintendent fired a gun out on the Banks and all the dhows and boats raced for the shore.[1]

The Arabs ran their boats up on to the sand and with a tremendous shouting rushed into the koddu carrying their oysters in great baskets. The koddu was an enormous fenced square enclosure with nine open huts running down it from end to end. Each hut was divided into compartments, and each boat as soon as it arrived had to bring in its load of oysters and deposit it in a compartment dividing it up into three equal heaps. The Koddu Superintendent, of whom I was one, then went round and chose two out of the three heaps as the Government's share, leaving the other heap to be gathered up by the divers and to be taken with a roar of shouting out of the koddu.

Later in the evening the Government's oysters were auctioned by the G.A. When the first divers rushed their shares out of the koddu, they were surrounded by a crowd of pearl dealers and merchants who bid against one another for the oysters. Those who succeeded in getting some, hurried away and opened the oysters to see whether the number and quality of the pearls which they con-

[1] Some of the boats were towed in by a Government steamer.

tained were above or below average. What they found in these samples determined the bidding at the Government auction in the evening. The method of extracting the pearls from the oysters was primitive and insanitary. The oysters were put into a canoe or dug-out and allowed to rot for several days; when the oysters had decayed, seawater was put into the canoe which was gently rocked and the seawater gradually poured off; there upon the bottom of the canoe was a sediment of sand, putrid oyster, and pearls. As the Fishery went on and the whole camp became full of thousands of putrid and putrescent oysters, a horrible smell hung over it and us night and day and myriads of flies swarmed over everything. Every particle of food had to be kept closely covered until the last moment before you popped it into your mouth.

John Scott, as A.G.A., was responsible for law and order in the camp, sat as Police Magistrate, and was Koddu Superintendent; I was Assistant Koddu Superintendent; Stevenson was Superintendent of Police. Stevenson and I shared a bungalow. I was also Additional Police Magistrate, and when I had time helped with the supervision of the camp. The work of the Koddu Superintendents was onerous and exhausting. In theory the fishing ended each day in the early afternoon, the dhows raced back before the wind blowing from the sea, the divers dumped their oysters and the Government had taken its share and the koddu was cleared by the late afternoon. This ideal timetable rarely worked out in practice. For the dhows to get back to the shore from the Banks reasonably early in the afternoon, they required a fairly brisk south-west wind. Very often they got a light or contrary wind or no wind at all, and they had to tack or even row. When this happened, the boats would drop in one by one all night long and even on into the following day.

At one time we were fishing a Bank nearly 20 miles away and the boats, with a favourable wind, took four or five hours to get in, but the wind was consistently unfavourable and day after day they took 12, 24, or even 36 hours to reach the shore. A Koddu Superintendent had to be in the koddu the whole time, keeping order among the hundreds of shouting, gesticulating Arabs in the light of flickering oil lamps and torches and taking over the Government's oysters. In the day one trudged up and down the koddu through the sand under a blazing sky. "It is like walking about hour after hour", I wrote in a letter, "in a hell twice as mad as the coaling at Port Said. It is merely coolie work supervising this and the counting and issuing of about one or two million oysters a day, for the Arabs will do anything if you hit them hard enough with a walking stick, an occupation in which I have been engaged for the most part of the last 3 days and nights." The heat and the flies made everyone feel ill and at the most hectic moment Stevenson went down with malaria and Scott was also ill. I was almost continually in the koddu night and day and, when not there, patrolling the camp or trying police court cases. In a letter to Lytton I wrote: "The work is consequently going on day and night and I have only been about 3 or 4 hours in bed out of the last 72."

I think that my recovery from typhoid had given me a new lease of life and, as I often said at the time, a new inside. I know I felt extraordinarily well and completely untirable. But I also experienced in the sands of Marich-chukaddi one of those sudden, instantaneous cures which at the moment seem a divine miracle and exhilarate one so that for a time one becomes immune to all the ills of the flesh. When I left Jaffna, I was suffering from an eczema which is very usual in Ceylon. But the heat and continual walking in the sand of the koddu made it infinitely worse and my thighs and scrotum were covered and inflamed with an intolerable rash. The pain and discomfort of walking about for five or six hours on end in the sun in this condition were appalling. I bore it for three or four days and then, after I left the koddu one morning, I went to the Medical Officer and asked him whether he could do anything. He gave me a lotion which I immediately put on. The result was, as I said, literally to me a miracle. When I put the lotion on I was in a raw and bleeding state, and I had to go back to the koddu in the afternoon. By that time, I was more or less comfortable—and I had been in acute discomfort for days—and when I left the koddu about midnight, I was recovered.

There was a great deal to be said against our rule of Ceylon, which, of course, was bleak "imperialism" or what is now fashionably called colonialism. One of the good things about it, however, was the extraordinary absence of the use of force in everyday life and government. Ceylon in 1906 was the exact opposite of a "police state". There were very few police and outside Colombo and Kandy not a single soldier. From the point of view of law and order nothing could have been more dangerously precarious than the Pearl Fishery camp, a temporary town of 30,000 or 40,000 men, many of whom were habitual criminals. As the Fishery went on, the town became fuller and fuller of a highly valuable form of property, pearls. There was one danger which was a perpetual nightmare to us and which I will deal with later, but apart from that we four civil servants never even thought about the possibility of our not being able to maintain law and order. And we were quite right. In the koddu we had an interpreter, some police constables, and a few Tamils whose duty it was to take over the Government's shares of the oysters and see that no one touched them. Otherwise I was single-handed and had to keep order among a thousand or more Arabs pouring into an enclosed space dimly lit, carrying heavy sacks and baskets of oysters, and all desperately anxious to find a good empty compartment and to get out of the koddu as quickly as possible with their share of oysters. At the time it seemed to me quite easy and natural to do this with a loud voice and a walking stick, though I was by nature, as I have already said more than once, a nervous and cowardly person.

The Arabs fascinated me, both in themselves and because of the contrast between them and the Tamils. The Tamil crowd was low in tone, rather timid, depressed and complaining in adversity. The Arab superficially was the exact opposite. At the end of the Fishery I went in a small steamer, packed with about 1,000 Arabs and Tamils, to Paumben in India. The men swarmed everywhere over all the decks and overflowed into the three small cabins and into the box of a saloon. The sea was rough all night and they were seasick most of the time. In a letter to Lytton describing this I contrasted the behaviour of the Semitic with that of the Dravidian, perhaps somewhat unfairly. The Tamils, I wrote, were "huddling together, squabbling and complaining, but the Arab is superb, he has the grand manner, absolutely saturnine, no fuss or excitement, but one could see when day broke that every Arab had room and to spare to stretch full length in his blanket on the deck."

The Arabs were not always calm; when they rushed up the beach with their great sacks of oysters, talking at the top of their voices, shouting, laughing, the noise was tremendous, and it was wonderful when above the tumult one heard a voice from the sea crying trailingly and melodiously "Ab-d-ul-la! Ab-d-ul-la!" The men of each boat always kept closely together, and among the Arabs were a certain number of Negroes, said to have been or even to be slaves. Every Arab seemed to have his own copper coffeepot. In one boat there was a gigantic Negro —he must have been six foot five inches or six foot six inches—he was wrapped about with several sacks, and, tied together with a rope, dangling and clattering on his back were always 15 or 20 copper coffeepots which he carried for his companions. One of the ways in which the Arab was different from the Tamil was the way in which he treated the white man in authority. The Tamil treated one as someone apart; he would never dream of touching one, for instance. The Arabs, on the other hand, although extremely polite, treated me as a fellow human being. If anything went wrong or there was a dispute which I had to settle, they would surround me and make long eloquent guttural speeches, and often if one of them got excited, he would put his hand on my shoulder to emphasize the torrent of his words. Once towards the end of the Fishery, when they all knew me well and I had got to know some of them quite well, one of them before he left the koddu rushed up to me, put one hand on my shoulder, made a short speech, and then took off his camel-hair head-dress and the nose-clip which hung round his neck and gave them to me.

It was this attitude of human equality which accounted for the fact, oddly enough, that I hit them with a walking stick, whereas in the whole of my time in Ceylon I never struck, or would have dared to strike, a Tamil or a Sinhalese. When all the boats were coming in together, the koddu became a struggling mass of packed human beings, Arabs hauling in their sacks of oysters from the beach or carrying them out to sell at the other end. To get through the crowd from compartment to compartment in order to see that the division of the oysters was properly made— as I had to do—I simply had to fight my way through, shouting "Get out of the way—get out of the way", and the Arabs were vastly amused when I used my walking stick to clear a passage through them.

One scene in the koddu, connected with the Arabs, of a very different kind, tragic and beautiful, I shall never forget. I had been in the koddu all night and the last Arabs and the last oysters were leaving in the early hours of the morning. I was just going to leave myself when an Arab came in from the beach and told me that one of his men had died when diving out on the banks and that the body and the rest of his crew were still on board. As small-pox had broken out in the camp, I kept all the Arabs on board and sent for the Medical Officer. When he came, I went down to the shore with him. Four men waded out to the boat: the corpse was lifted out and placed on their shoulders. Forty years ago, when the scene was still vividly in my memory, I wrote down a description of it, and I think it is better to quote it here verbatim rather than to write it afresh all over again. The four men "waded back slowly; the feet of the dead man stuck out, toes pointing up, very stark over the shoulders of the men in front. The body was laid on the sand. The bearded face of the dead man looked very calm, very dignified in the faint light." The doctor made his examination, and when at last he said it was not smallpox, I told the sheik in charge of the boat that he could remove the body. An Arab, the brother of the dead man, was sitting on the sand near his head. "He covered himself with sackcloth. I heard him weeping. It was very silent, very cold and still on the shore in the early dawn. A tall figure stepped forward, it was the Arab sheik, the leader of the boat. He laid his hand on the head of the weeping man and spoke to him calmly, eloquently, compassionately. I didn't understand Arabic, but I could understand what he was saying. The dead man had lived, had worked, had died. He had died working, without suffering, as men should desire to die. He had left a son behind him. The speech went on calmly, eloquently, I heard continually the word Khallas—all is finished. I watched the figures outlined against the grey sky—the long lean outline of the corpse with the toes sticking up so straight and stark, the crouching huddled figure of the weeping man, and the tall upright sheik standing by his side. They were motionless, sombre, mysterious, part of the grey sea, of the grey sky.

"Suddenly the dawn broke red in the sky. The sheik stopped, motioned silently to the four men. They lifted the dead man on to their shoulders. They moved away down the shore by the side of the sea which began to stir under the cold wind. By their side walked the sheik, his hand laid gently on the brother's arm. I watched them move away, silent, dignified. And over the shoulders of the men I saw the feet of the dead man with the toes sticking up straight and stark."

There was so much work and so much illness during the two months of the Fishery that we had very little time for social life. It was rare for us all to be free of an evening for dinner and bridge and "Funiculi, funicula", which

The author in Jaffna

Fisherman on Jaffna lagoon

Jaffna Hindu temple

PEARL FISHERY

Arab divers with nose clips
Preparing to dive

PEARL FISHERY

Boats arriving from the banks
Carrying the oysters into the koddu

The Empress Eugénie

ABOVE: *The author with the Ratemahatmayas outside the Kandy kachcheri.* RIGHT: *Fetching water from the tank of a village in the jungle* (BY COURTESY OF ANGELA DAUGHARTY)

The author with Hambantota kachcheri staff, mudaliyars,
muhandiram, and Engelbrecht

The author with Hambantota kachcheri staff and Father Cooreman

was what Mrs. Lewis pined for. This was no doubt a pity for we all got on very well together. Scott, the A.G.A., who had been a scholar of King's, I had known for some time and liked. Stevenson was an amusing Irishman and talked incessantly like an Irishman in a novel; he was also extremely able and became Sir Malcolm Stevenson, K.C.M.G., Governor of Cyprus. A curious incident happened to us one night. We had been dining with the G.A. and were walking back to our bungalow. The night was very dark and we had a boy with us lighting our way over the sand with a dim hurricane lamp. Stevenson was discoursing to me and at one point stopped characteristically and faced me so that the fountain of words should be as little impeded as possible. We stood facing each other a few feet apart and, as he talked he slowly twirled round and round, a few inches in front of my nose and of his, a walking stick. Suddenly the stick caught on something on the ground and whizzed it up in the air between us. As it fell back on the ground, Stevenson brought his stick down on it. The boy rushed up with the hurricane lamp and there upon the ground by our feet was a tic-polonga, a Russell's viper, one of the deadliest of Ceylon snakes.

I always liked the job of patrolling the camp late at night. One or other of us invariably did this to see that the police were on their beats and awake and that nothing suspicious was going on. The danger which perpetually hung over our heads was that some gang of malefactors would set fire to the camp and then, in the panic which followed, start looting. This had been tried more than once and had in fact a year or two before succeeded. In a fresh wind the wood and cadjan huts went up in flames like tinder and on that occasion nearly the whole camp was destroyed in an hour or two. When one patrolled, however late it was, there were always people walking about or sitting in front of their huts. Very often a pearl dealer or merchant would invite one to sit down with him and have a small cup of Turkish coffee. As the Fishery went on and they got to know me, they would show me some of the pearls they had got from purchased oysters or bought from other people. Once I saw an almost naked coolie walking round the dealers' quarter, clutching something tightly in his hand. I guessed it to be a pearl and asked him to let me see it. He opened his hand for a second, just long enough for me to see one of the largest and most perfect pearls I saw during the Fishery.

The Fishery came to an end early in April and I returned to Jaffna via Colombo. I had been away from it to all intents and purposes for the better part of six months, ever since I was stricken with typhoid, and I found changes in it which changed the rhythm of my life. To start with I lived with the Assistant Conservator of Forests, G. D. Templer, in a largish bungalow down on the shore of the lagoon or sea. It was an official bungalow with the offices of the Forest Department in a building at the back. Templer shared my liking of all kinds of animals and we acquired quite a menagerie, beginning with five dogs and eventually including a leopard, a spotted deer, and a monkey. The deer roamed about the large compound, the monkey when we were not in the bungalow was chained to a pillar of the verandah and usually sat on the roof which the chain was long enough to allow him to reach.

The leopard had been found when a cub in the jungle by a Forest Officer who gave him to Templer. When he was small, the dogs were very fond of him and they used to romp with one another up and down the verandah. He was also great friends with the deer; he used to stalk the deer and suddenly jump on his back with his foreleg over the shoulder in true leopard manner, and the deer would then shake him off and butt him round and round the compound, both of them obviously enjoying the game. The leopard came to a sad end. As he grew up, he failed to realize his own strength. He would playfully bat a dog as he always had done, but he was now so strong that a playful tap sent the unfortunate dog head over heels, and, when he was some way from being full grown, none of the dogs would go near him. Now when he caught one playfully by the ankle or tried to jump on to one's lap, it was rather painful. The clerks in the Forest Office and our boys became frightened of him, and we had to keep him tied up to a coconut tree whenever we were not in the bungalow. He was a very affectionate animal and the only living creature to which he showed any positive dislike was the monkey. One day when Templer and I were out, he broke his rope, climbed on to the roof, and caught the monkey. The Forest head clerk bravely beat him off the monkey with a broom. When we came back, we found the monkey badly torn, but we doctored him and he recovered. A week or so later, when we got up one morning, we found the leopard dead—his rope had got over one of the fronds of the coconut tree and he was hanged. It is just possible that climbing about on the tree, he slipped and hanged himself; but I have little doubt that his death was contrived by the clerks and our servants.

The deer also occasioned a tragedy, which might have been very serious. He was a beautiful and charming beast; he had a passion for cigarettes and tobacco, and whenever we had a meal, he would come up on to the veran-dah or into the sitting-room and wait patiently by the table until he was given a cigarette. But as he and his horns grew, though he remained very affectionate to me and would let me do anything with him, his temper with other people became uncertain. One afternoon when I returned from the kachcheri I found a small crowd in the compound, a woman and three children weeping and wailing, and the latrine coolie lying on the ground with a nasty wound in his thigh. The deer had attacked him, knocking him down, and gored him. I took him off to the hospital and, though seriously ill for a time, he recovered. In the evening reluctantly we shot the deer.

I do not know why I am so fond of animals. They give me the greatest pleasure both emotionally and intellectually. I get deep affection for cats and dogs, and indeed for almost every kind of animal which I have kept. But I also derive very great pleasure from understanding them, *their* emotions and *their* minds. They are, too, as I have said, usually amazingly beautiful. I was always condemned by Lytton on this account for being sentimental and many people, particularly intellectuals, would agree with him. I daresay that to some extent they are right. I daresay that there is sentimentality in my affection for my dog and my cats, for the leopard who hurled himself into my lap, for the marmoset who lived with me for five years. But I think there is also something more to it. If you really understand an animal so that he gets to trust you completely and, within his limits, understands you, there grows up between you affection of a purity and simplicity which seems to me peculiarly satisfactory. There is also a cosmic strangeness about animals which always fascinates me and gives to my affection for them a mysterious depth or background. I do not think that from the human point of view there is any sense in the universe if you face it with the gloves and the tinted spectacles off, but it is obvious that messiahs, prophets, Buddhas, Gods and Sons of Gods, philosophers, by confining their attention to man, have invented the most elaborate cosmological fantasies which have satisfied or deceived millions of people about the meaning of the universe and their own position in it. But the moment you try to fit into these fantasies my cat, my dog, my leopard, my marmoset, with their strange minds, fears, affections —their souls if there is such a thing as a soul—you see that they make nonsense of all philosophies and religions.

Before I leave this subject of animals, which, I know, will irritate many of my readers, I want to describe a curious incident which I saw take place in the bungalow by the sea. I have often heard of people who have a magnetic power over animals, but this is the only time in my life that I have seen an exhibition of it. Templer had a fox terrier bitch which normally was completely good-tempered and obedient. She had a litter of puppies in a basket in the corner of our bathroom and the moment they were born she went madly savage, refusing to allow anyone, including Templer, to come into the room. The moment that Templer tried to go in she flew at him and in the narrow space he found it impossible to get hold of her without being severely bitten. I tried with the same result. Next day an Irrigation Engineer who was in charge of a large irrigation work in the Northern Province looked in on us. He was a big, dark, gentle, shy, silent man called Harward. We told him what was happening in the bathroom and he asked us what we wanted done with the bitch and her puppies. We said we wanted to get her and her basket into another small room so that we could use the bathroom. He said that he thought he could

manage that. He opened the door of the bathroom. The
bitch immediately sat up in the basket growling; Harward walked straight up to her, patted her on the head
and made her lie down, and carried the basket with the
whole family quietly in it into the other room.

The bungalow by the sea was in many ways a very
pleasant place. It is true that Jaffna is upon the sea, but
the sea looks and behaves as if it is a lagoon. This is
because the town and peninsula are almost completely
shut in on the west by islands. Every now and again I
had to sail out to these islands in a Government boat, a
kind of dinghy, on Customs duty, and all along the shore
of the long island facing Jaffna one could see a long pink
line of flamingos wading in the shallow waters. On the
sandy shore in front of our bungalow there was practically
no rise and fall of tide and rarely a wave. There was
always a strong smell of sea and seaweed. Not very far
from us at that time lived two young English girls with
their widowed mother. They used to take a walk on the
beach in the (comparative) cool of the evening, and
Templer and I got into the habit of joining them. One of
them, Gwen, was pretty, lively, sweet-natured and I
became fond of her and she of me. In 1906 it was highly
improper in Ceylon that these two young women should
wander about on the beach with two young men after
dark and I often pondered over why their mother, a most
respectable lady, allowed it. After the fierce heat of the
day a gentle, languid, and pleasant melancholy would
settle over the lagoon and over us as we lay on the seaweedy sand platonically—if that is the right word—in
each other's arms. For many years, long after she married
and had a family, she used occasionally to write to me, and
even up to today whenever I suddenly get the strong

smell of seaweed, as in the town of Worthing, I get a vivid vision of Gwen and the sands of Jaffna.

Besides Gwen I have a curious memory of another woman upon those sands. One day I had been away for over 24 hours from Jaffna on an enquiry. When I got back in the late afternoon and walked into my room in the bungalow, I was wearing a pair of white flannel trousers. Three minutes later I looked down and saw that the trousers half-way up to the knee had turned black. They were black with fleas and the whole floor of the room was black with thousands of fleas. I dashed into the compound, tore off the trousers and shouted to my boy to bring me a clean pair. Then I wandered out on to the beach and stood there in the depths of gloom, for I did not see how I could possibly get rid of such a plague and swarm. As I stood there, a very old, bent Tamil woman of the fisher caste hobbled by. To my immense surprise she stopped, came up to me, and said: "Why is your honour so sad?" "I am sad", I said, "because I have just come back to my bungalow after being away out there for a day or two, and now I find the floor of my room black with thousands of fleas." "If your honour will wait here for a little," she said, "I will bring you something which will rid the house of the fleas. There is no need for your honour to be sad. We will get rid of the fleas." She hobbled away and after five or ten minutes re-appeared with a handful of some herb. She told me to take it and make my boy spread it on newspaper on the floor of the bungalow and set fire to the paper and that when the herb burnt all the fleas would leave the house. I thanked her and did what she said. To my great astonishment, the thing worked; the miracle was accomplished; half an hour later there was not a flea in the place.

Although the white population of Jaffna was so small, it contained a high percentage of curious characters. One of the most curious exhibits was Sir William Twynam, K.C.M.G. When I knew him he was 79 years old, living in a house not far from our bungalow on the seashore, a straight-backed, lean, scraggy old man, with a skimpy beard, with that slightly wild, worried look in the eye which you see in many bad-tempered horses. If you had put him into armour with a lance in his hand he would have passed anywhere as Don Quixote, though I think he was the last person to tilt at windmills. He had retired after 50 years in the Ceylon Civil Service, all of it spent in Jaffna, and over 40 years as Government Agent, Northern Province. On his retirement he bought a house and continued to live in Jaffna. It was said that he had started life in the Navy and came out to Ceylon as a midshipman on a man-of-war. His boat put into Trincomalee and he was sent ashore with a company of men to buy provisions. They got into a row with some of the inhabitants and the midshipman and his men fought their way through a hostile crowd into a Hindu temple where they were besieged. They were eventually rescued by an armed force under a lieutenant. Twynam was taken to Colombo, court-martialled, and summarily dismissed from his ship and from the Royal Navy. He was stranded in Colombo practically penniless.

At this time the Government Agent at Jaffna was P. A. Dyke, known as the Rajah of the North, for he ruled his province as a paternal despot. It was said that he was over 40 years G.A. in Jaffna, so that the Northern Province had only two G.A.'s in 80 years. In 40 years he went back on leave to England only once, and the story was that when he got out of the train at Victoria and took a fourwheeler, the cabman was rude to him and he was so infuriated that he immediately returned to Jaffna and never left it again. Dyke, hearing of Twynam's plight and thinking that he had been harshly treated, offered him a place in the Civil Service in the Northern Province. Twynam accepted and spent the remainder of his life in Jaffna.

In my day every new civil servant when he came to Jaffna went and paid his respects to the great man. Whenever I went he was holding a kind of small durbar of chief headmen, for he was still a kind of underground power in the peninsula. He was a formidable old man though quite friendly to me. I never had the courage to ask him whether it was true that he had been dismissed from the Navy. But he did tell me one day that when he first came out he had spent some time in Colombo and had seen strange sights at a military parade on Galle Face. The parade took place at midday in the hottest season of the year and the troops wore thick stocks round their necks and high collars. Dozens of men fainted and were just pulled out of the line and just left on the ground to recover—or not to recover for, according to Twynam, it was quite common for ten or twelve men to die of sunstroke during a parade in Colombo in the 1840's.

A major change for me in Jaffna, when I returned to it from the Pearl Fishery, was that Lewis, the G.A., was transferred to Kandy and the Central Province, and his place was taken by Ferdinando Hamlyn Price. Price, who was 51 and had had 25 years in the Civil Service, was a very odd character. He was a Welshman, and looked exactly like the man whom every foreigner regards as the typical Englishman, and indeed there are hundreds of men in the British Isles who at the age of 50 look like

F. H. Price—tall, thin, athletic looking, baldish, with a long hatchet-face, an impassive, unflinching, implacable eye, an air of natural unshakable superiority and of good-humoured tolerance of so many obviously inferior (but well-meaning, so far as they go) persons. He was a terrific snob and was—or believed himself to be—a Welsh land-owner and gentleman—and he believed that practically no one else in Ceylon was a gentleman. He had three passions: regularity in his everyday life, horses, and golf. He was reputed in the Service to be very slightly mad, and I think that perhaps he was. As a young man he used to race in Colombo, riding his own horses. One day in a race on Galle Face the girth of his saddle broke and he was flung off on to his head. It is true that he had a bad scar and dent on his forehead and it was said that after the accident he became slightly mad.

The above description would on the face of it make Price out to have been an unpleasant man. But in fact he wasn't, for in human beings the character is rarely all black or all white. Price was absurd and, when he was nasty, he could be very very nasty. But he had some very good points and in the end I came to like him and he liked me. In the business of life, using the word business in a strict sense, I owe a great deal to him, for he taught me very valuable lessons and methods in administration, lessons and methods which are applicable to all *business*. He was congenitally and incorrigibly lazy, and, as soon as he found that I was extremely competent and the opposite to him so far as laziness was concerned, he made me do all my work and nearly all of his. His day and mine were regulated by a rigid iron routine. He did not come to the kachcheri, but did his work—such as it was—in his house. All the Government business and papers and persons had to come through me and practically the only person whom he would ever actually see was myself. If anyone came for an interview, they had to see me and, if they wanted to go beyond me to him, they had to put what they wanted to say in writing. This applied even to Government servants. He would never see the head clerk or the kachcheri Mudlayar, who was a kind of A.D.C. to the G.A. and head of all the headmen—even these officers if they wanted to say anything to him had to put it in writing.

Price was not one of those people who lay down general principles for life, business or anything else, but I learnt from him two golden rules which ever since I have found applicable in many departments of life. The first is never to use two words where you can express your meaning clearly in one. Price himself seemed to me to write on the principle that he could express his meaning in one word where anyone else would require a minimum of ten. The second rule is that, both in business and in private life, 99 out of every 100 letters received by you, which require an answer, should be answered on the day on which you receive them. This is, I believe, one of the foundations of office efficiency and one of the great discoveries for saving one time and worry. Ever since the year 1906 I have practised it in my private life and have insisted upon it in every Government office or business for which I have been responsible. Whenever I came new into an office in Ceylon, I would find 10, 20, or 30 great files waiting on my table to be dealt with and only 5 to 10 per cent of the ordinary routine letters would be answered on the day they were received. The average time for a person to get a reply to a letter of his from a Government office would probably be a week to ten days. On my second day in the office I always sent for the head clerk and said to him: "Every letter received in this kachcheri after this week must be answered on the day of its receipt unless it is waiting for an order from me or from the G.A." The answer of the head clerk was always that in this office the number of letters received daily is so large that it would be totally impossible to answer them in the same day. And the answer to that was: "You are receiving in this office 500 letters a day, or 13,000 a month. Nine out of ten of the letters which you answer today were received in the office five or six days ago. But the number of unanswered letters at the beginning of the month is on the average the same as the number of unanswered letters at the end of the month. So you are in fact answering about 500 letters every day, for otherwise the number of unanswered letters would continually increase and eventually you would be answering letters today which you received months and years ago. Therefore if you once catch up—as I insist upon your doing—you will find that you save yourself and everyone else an immense amount of time and worry." I then took the head clerk with me and visited every room in the kachcheri examining the table of every clerk to see exactly what he was doing, what letters he had on his table unanswered and on what date they were received. This was a formidable undertaking, particularly in a kachcheri like Kandy where there must have been over 100 clerks, and I went down into the very bowels of the earth, into that bottomless pit (in those days) of official darkness and despair, the Record Department, the registration and filing department. I do not believe that any civil servant had ever before really inspected the filing departments of the three kachcheris in which I served. They were all monuments of official in-

competence, bottlenecks of delay—in the Kandy kachcheri there were mountains of unregistered and unfiled
letters and minutes.

I told the head clerk that he should let everyone know
that I proposed to inspect the whole kachcheri and every
clerk's desk in the same way monthly until I found that
the Record Department was up to date and every letter
was being as a general rule answered on the day of its
receipt. All this made me extremely unpopular and I got
the reputation among the Tamils, and later among the
Sinhalese, of being a strict and ruthless civil servant. But
in every place I insisted upon and succeeded in making a
domestic revolution, and even in Kandy, at the end of my
time there, letters were being answered on the day of
their receipt. I don't think I was ever popular with my
office staff; they thought me too severe and too opinionated.
But as time went by they completely changed their view
of my methods of business organization, and nearly all of
them agreed that my revolution had not only enormously
increased efficiency but made their own work easier. This
is not wishful thinking and complacency, for I have two
pieces of evidence. When I left Jaffna for Kandy in 1907,
one of the leading lawyers, a respectable and respected
man in Jaffna, V. Casippillai, who had nothing to gain by
flattering me, wrote to me:

                                          Jaffna
Dear Sir,   23rd August, 1907
    I very much regret that I was not able to have
seen and bid you goodbye ere your departure from
Jaffna, as I was laid up with a sharp attack of bronkitis
[sic] from which I have not quite recovered yet. Very
few here worked as hard as you have done or earned a

reputation for more conscientious discharge of duties
and I can bear testimony to the fact that very many of
your subordinates who had evinced much displeasure
at your relations with them at the outset had to confess
that they had never had a superior who exacted so much
work and at the same time treated them so kindly,
holding the balance between all parties—justice being
your motto.

Wishing you a long and prosperous career
I remain
Yours truly
V Casippillai

The second piece of evidence came from Kandy. The
amount of Government work in Kandy was very heavy
all through the kachcheri and I had a severe struggle
against the head clerk and others before I was able to put
through my revolution. But once the revolution was made
and delays got rid of in the office, the more the work the
more effective is efficiency. One day after I had been
transferred from Kandy to Hambantota, I had to go up
country on official business. In the late afternoon I got
into the train at Colombo for Kandy and, seeing the head
clerk of the Kandy kachcheri on the platform, I asked him
to come in my carriage and have a chat. We talked about
old times and then suddenly he said to me that when I
first came to the kachcheri and said that everything must
be brought up to date and that practically all letters must
be answered at once, there had very nearly been an open
revolt against me. Nobody in the office, including himself,
had believed the thing in the least degree possible. But
everyone, including himself, agreed that, once the change
had been made, the thing had proved to be feasible and

everyone's work became easier. Five minutes after this, to me, eminently satisfactory testimonial, I literally saved the head clerk's life. Half-way to Kandy the train was drawing into a station, I suppose it was Ambepussa, and before it had stopped he impetuously opened the carriage door in order to get out and buy himself an orange or plantain. His foot slipped and he fell between the train and the platform, or would have done if I had not caught him round the waist and held him up until the train stopped.

My unpopularity in Jaffna was not undeserved. I meant well by the people of Jaffna, but, even when my meaning was well, and also right—not always the case or the same thing—my methods were too ruthless, too much the "strong man". The difficulties and the friction made me for the first time dimly perceive the problems of the imperialist. It is curious, looking back, to see how long it took me to become fully conscious of my position as a ruler of subject peoples. But I remember the moment when for the first time I became fully aware of it and the awareness brought my first doubts whether I wanted to rule other people, to be an imperialist and proconsul. The Jaffna Tamil Association twice reported me to the Governor and asked for my dismissal—an unusual distinction for a civil servant of only two years' service. In both cases the G.A. was directed to call upon me for an explanation.

The first case arose from an order which I had posted in the verandah of the kachcheri. The amount of spitting which went on in the verandah was extremely unpleasant. The notice said that spitting on the verandah was forbidden and the peons were ordered to turn out anyone who spat. One day one of my own clerks spat and I told him to clean the spot. "He refused", I wrote at the time, "but, when he saw I meant it, he did it. Of course I knew he was of a caste to hate doing it, but he was also a person who wanted a lesson given to him. There are other things like that: I expect a row." The way I did this was, of course, crudely wrong, but the Governor accepted my explanation and there was no row. But I wrote, also at the time, the following about the complaints of the Tamils: "They don't like the 'strong measures' of Price and myself, and so of course they take the paying line that we are anti-native. In my case they have pitched on things which are of course not anti-native but in the main true."

In their second complaint the Jaffna Association pitched on something which in fact was not true. They said that one of their most respected members, Mr. Harry Sanderasekara, a well-known lawyer, had been deliberately hit in the face by the Office Assistant, Mr. Leonard Woolf. Mr. Sanderasekara had been driving in his trap down the main street of Jaffna and he met the G.A., Mr. Price, and the O.A., Mr. Woolf, who were riding up the street in the opposite direction. As they passed one another, Mr. Woolf turned his horse and deliberately hit Mr. Sanderasekara in the face with his riding whip.

When I first read this document, I was dismayed, because I could not understand how or why such an accusation could have been made against me. I knew and liked Sanderasekara and had had business with him several times in kachcheri and Court on a friendly basis. Then suddenly I remembered vividly an incident which seemed to explain his misunderstanding and accusation. Shortly after Price took over as G.A., he and I were riding up the main street of the town, and, when we got to the top of it where it debouched into the esplanade, I asked him to stop and look back down the street, for, if he did so, he would see clearly how people had encroached upon the old line of the street by building verandahs and stoeps out on to the highway. I remembered the long straight street in the glare and dust, the white houses and verandahs, and women's heads peering through blinds or round doors to see what the white men were stopping for. I remembered that my horse had been restless, continually fidgeting and turning round and round as I pointed out with my riding whip to Ferdinando Hamlyn Price the old line of the street. And then I suddenly remembered that at some moment as my horse was dancing about, I had caught a glimpse out of the corner of my eye of a trap with Mr. Harry Sanderasekara sitting in it.

I gave my official explanation in writing to His Excellency the Governor and to the Central Government in Colombo. I said that I had never deliberately hit Mr. Sanderasekara or anyone else in Jaffna or anywhere else in the world with a riding whip. But I did remember how restive my horse had been as I pointed down the street with my whip, and I could only assume that, as the horse wheeled round, Mr. Sanderasekara was driving past and the whip, without my being aware of it, had passed near his face. The Governor and the Government accepted my explanation, but I doubted—and doubt—whether the Tamil Association and Mr. Sanderasekara believed or accepted it. It shocked me that these people should think that, as a white man and a ruler of Ceylon, I should consider the brown man, the Tamil, to be one of "the lesser breeds" and deliberately hit him in the face with my riding whip to show him that he must behave himself and keep in his place. For that is what all this meant. And perhaps for the first time I felt a twinge of doubt in my imperialist soul, a doubt whether we were not in the wrong, and the Jaffna Tamil Association and Mr. Sander-asekara in the right, not right in believing that I would and had hit him in the face, but right in feeling that my sitting on a horse arrogantly in the main street of their town was as good as a slap in the face.

As time went on, I spent more and more of my time with Price and Mrs. Price. They made me lunch with them every day when the kachcheri was open. Mrs. Price was the exact opposite of Mrs. Lewis. She was a real Victorian lady, daughter of the head of the Natural History Museum, far away now in Cromwell Road and Queens Gate and the quiet security of Kensington. I think that the life with Price and Ceylon into which Fate had cruelly pitched her terrified her, but, being a lady, she concealed it, except for the unhappiness terribly stamped upon her face. She was rather silent and extremely nervous. The curious thing about her was her hand-writing which was very bold and beautiful, and she always signed her letters as if with conviction and enthusiasm very large:

Yours very sincerely,
Geraldine Rose Price.

She was an eminently nice person, and, if one had ever been able to get through the impenetrable reserve, her ladylikeness, her deep distrust of human beings, I am sure that one would have found an exceptionally sweet nature. I came to like her very much, and she liked me and every year after I left Jaffna I was asked by her to come and spend Christmas and the New Year with them. The following letter gives, I think, the flavour of her character:

THE OLD PARK,
JAFFNA KACHCHERI,
JAFFNA.
30th October, 1907.

Dear Mr. Woolf,

If you have not made any other plans for Christmas, we wondered whether you would like to come back to Jaffna? If so, we should be so pleased if you will stay with us and hope you will be able to manage to spend both Christmas and the New Year here. We could then have plenty of golf, and perhaps our new greens will be ready that we are beginning to make here.

Jaffna is looking very green now, very different to when we went away. No calamity happened while we were away, and we found all the animals well on our return and we ourselves were much refreshed by the little change. Twilight says that he also hopes you will be able to spend Christmas here.

Yours very sincerely,
Geraldine Rose Price.

P.S. Could you tell me something about Mr. Wedderburn? I was wondering whether you would care to bring him with you. Would he do? We have never seen him.

G. R. P.

The more I saw of Price, the more strange I found him. It fascinated me to watch that eye of his which positively glittered and with which he "fixed" his victim in order that by its help he could "deal with" people, as he called it. He was one of the few people I have known who had absolutely no heart: his harshness was incredible, as I once wrote to Lytton, and with his astonishing grasp of

115

situations it was only his absolute lack of imagination which made him obviously not a great man. He suffered too from being a kind of aristocrat and a schoolboy who had never grown up into the world of reality and 1906. He had an instinctive grasp of a "situation" and of the person with whom he was "dealing". I got on well with him because I understood him and he knew that I understood him and that it was no good his trying to "deal with" me for I was impervious to the glittering eye. Also I did an enormous amount of work for him and was as intelligent as he was.

When he found out the kind of person I was, he tried to absorb me into their life, and life for the Prices was a fantastic routine. To some extent he succeeded, though I always obstinately refused to be really absorbed. The routine was as follows, so far as I was concerned. I went to the kachcheri very early, attended to the tappal (the daily mountain of letters), prepared the papers which I considered I should discuss with him and took them over to him in his house. Having settled with him what should be done, I returned to the kachcheri and worked until one o'clock. At one o'clock to the second, I went across to The Old Park and lunched with the Prices. The lunch was practically always the same and we drank Madeira, a wine which Price thought that a gentleman should drink for lunch in whatever climate he might live, a wine which I think is uninteresting and which no one, whether a gentleman or no gentleman—for there was one of each at Price's table—or indeed a lady, should drink in a climate like Jaffna's. At lunch conversation was easy, but fundamentally dull, as indeed nearly all conversation was in Ceylon. All shop was forbidden in the presence of a lady. Price had a passion for betting—he would bet on anything—and I have a milder, not passion, but liking for any kind of gamble. Every day we had a sweepstake on guessing what the rainfall had been in the previous 24 hours. As Office Assistant, I was administrative maid of all works, and among my infinite duties I was responsible for the elementary meteorological records, including the daily rainfall statistics. So every morning, when I went over to lunch, I had in my pocket a paper recording the rainfall during the 24 hours ending at noon on the previous day. Mrs. Price had in her possession three pieces of paper on which each of us had at the previous day's lunch written what we thought the rainfall of the previous 24 hours had been; she also held three rupees, for each of us had deposited a stake of one rupee. The one whose guess was nearest to the actual rainfall pocketed the three rupees, and we then proceeded with the same routine all over again. As the rainfall for day after day between the monsoons was always nil, the routine was nearly always crazy.

I should like here to leave Price for a moment at his lunch and say something about rain. We do not know what rain is when we live in a place like England. In a place like Jaffna, and again in Hambantota, where I spent my last three years of Ceylon life, it is strange and entrancing. For weeks and months, between the South-West and North-East Monsoons, there is no rain at all—a clear sky, a burning south-west wind day after day sweeping across the brown parched earth. Then one evening some time in October a cloud appears upon the horizon. It does not reach one and fades away and next day the glaring sky and parching wind is on one again. This goes on for a day or two. And then suddenly the rain comes, and you hear it coming from miles away in the breathless evening, the patter patter patter of the rain on the palms and trees, creeping slowly towards one until suddenly the sun is blotted out and with a rush and a roar of wind it is upon one, a deluge of water from heaven. Every year that this happened, it seemed to me more and more miraculous, for the whole earth changed around one in an hour. I remember one year riding in the morning from my bungalow on the seashore to the kachcheri through a dead brown world. Everything was completely dried up, not a sign or sound of life anywhere, not a drop of water, not a speck of mud in any ditch or pond. While I was working at the kachcheri, the monsoon broke, the heavens opened, and I rode back in drenching rain through a world which had completely changed in an hour. The ditches were rushing rivers; the ponds were full, the earth was already turning green, the swish of the rain upon the trees was terrific, but deafening, drowning all other noises was the ecstatic chorus of millions of frogs from every ditch and pond and field and compound, a wild, mad, maddening, corybantic, croaking and creaking orgasm of sound and of wet, wallowing frogs.

To return to Price, after lunch I returned to the kachcheri. At half-past four or five, I went and had tea with the Prices, and then rode to the esplanade. On the esplanade we had made a primitive and not very interesting golf course. Price and I played golf. Mrs. Price sometimes walked with us and sometimes went for a ride with her dog Twilight. I had given Twilight to Mrs. Price and they were devotedly inseparable until he was killed and eaten by a leopard in the Mannar jungle before their eyes. He was a white whippet-like dog of dubious parentage on the father's side, his mother belonging to me. He once performed on the Jaffna esplanade a feat which, if I had not seen it, I should not have thought possible. There were usually on the esplanade little companies of five or six crows foraging, and Twilight would rush at them and send them swirling up into the air. One evening as they flew over his head he made one enormous leap into the air and caught a crow by its two feet and pulled it down and killed it.

Golf was to Price what Communion Service and its ritual are, I imagine, to a High Church parson. He was only a very moderately good player and so was I. As I have already said, I like all games and I like to play them seriously if I play them at all. But I would never put golf very high in the hierarchy of good games; it is too slowly long drawn out and therefore the anger against one's opponent, which in tennis and rackets, for instance, merely adds an occasional, momentary spur to one's efforts or exhaustion, in golf is apt to smoulder unpleasantly and sadistically. Price played it without any overt anger, but with cold and implacable seriousness. He induced me to order a set of clubs from Scotland, from the famous player and club maker, Auchterlonie.

In August 1906, the Assistant Government Agent, Mannar, was ill and took a month's leave and I was sent to Mannar to act for him. I was extremely pleased, partly to get away from Jaffna by myself for a month, and partly because it was almost unheard of for anyone with only a year and a half's experience to be appointed A.G.A. I enjoyed that month enormously. The Mannar District was 400 square miles in extent. It consisted almost entirely of uninhabited jungle; the only town was Mannar on the island of Mannar, where was the kachcheri, the Residency, and the Court. The island is really one of the islands which form Adam's Bridge between Ceylon and

India and is connected with the Ceylon mainland by a causeway.

I was the only white man in the 400 square miles of the District, and here for the first time I learnt the profound happiness of complete solitude. For a month I never spoke to anyone except clerks, headmen, Tamil villagers, and my own Tamil servants. My life and my work were entirely my own responsibility and there was no one whom I could consult about anything connected with either. I think this kind of complete solitude, with the necessity of relying absolutely upon oneself and one's own mind, is, when one is young, extremely good for one. I experienced it again during my three years in the Hambantota District. I acquired a taste for it which I have never lost, not for the permanent solitude of the hermit, or even for long periods of it, but for interludes of complete isolation. Even today, when evening falls and the door is shut in the street or in the village, and all life except my own and my dog's and my cat's is for the moment excluded, and for the moment there is cessation of the incessant fret and interruption of other people and outside existence, I enjoy the wordless and soundless meditation and the savour of one's own unhurried existence, and psychologically I am almost back again in the empty silent Residencies of Mannar and Hambantota or camping in the thick uninhabited jungles.

I learnt a great deal in my month as A.G.A. I spent most of my time riding about the District, exploring the jungles of the mainland and the small island of Mannar itself. The island is 18 miles in length and about two miles across. I had a curious expedition when I had to go and hold a land enquiry about 14 miles from Mannar town and about five miles from the other end of the island.

I arranged to sleep in a tiny bungalow on an estate belonging to the Chief Headman, and I rode there in the morning, my luggage and servants and food going on in a bullock cart. There were no proper roads, only sandy tracks. The enquiry ended in the late afternoon and I decided to ride to the northern tip of the island before dark and look across Adam's Bridge. At the tip of the island is Talaimannar and there I came upon an extraordinary spectacle, the graves of Adam and Eve. The graves were two enormous, smooth mounds of sand side by side, each about 30 yards long, five yards in width, and about two or three foot high in the centre. Each of them was completely covered from end to end with a white cotton sheet. They were surrounded by a large enclosure of wooden fences with a gate at one end in charge of three Muhammadans. It was they who told me that these mounds were the graves of Adam and Eve and that they would very much like me to come inside if I would take my shoes off. I tied my horse to the palisade, took off my shoes, and went through the gate. There was very nearly a strange catastrophe. I heard behind me a shout of horror and, turning round, saw my dog trying to follow me into the enclosure. I was just in time to stop him and make him lie down by the horse outside. Thus were the graves of our first parents saved by a hair's breadth from defilement by the dog of an infidel. Everyone was delighted, and in the small crowd, which, as always in Ceylon, had appeared out of nowhere and the wilderness of sand and was now following me, there were smiles and shaking of heads and lifting of hands. It was a red letter day for the 22 inhabitants of Talaimannar as well as for the acting A.G.A.

The acting A.G.A.'s adventures were not over. I stayed talking to the Muhammadans about the graves so long that, when I got on my horse and started to ride back to the place where I was to sleep, I found that I had left it much too late. Darkness began to fall and soon I had completely lost my way. The sandy track in the wilderness of sand was quite invisible and there were no villages and no inhabitants. All I could do was to look at the stars and ride south and trust to luck. My horse then performed one of those curious feats of instinct which always astonish me. He suddenly insisted upon going off at a right angle from the direction in which I was riding him. As I had no idea where I was and he seemed to know where he was, I let him have his head. After a mile or so he brought me straight to my carts and servants and bungalow and dinner. He had never been in that bit of country in his life before and he only stopped for two or three hours in the morning near the bungalow, but on a moonless night, across trackless sand, he had smelt or sensed a mile off his horsekeeper and his food and made off unhesitating, undeviating towards them. The bungalow was little more than a one-roomed hut with a tiled roof and I slept on my camp bed under a mosquito curtain. I always sleep well anywhere, but I was vaguely conscious of half waking up occasionally during the night to hear a strange persistent whirring noise in the room. It was due to hundreds of bats flying backwards and forwards in the small room, and, when I got up in the morning, my watch on a stool by the side of the bed was no longer visible for it was coated over completely with bats' dung, and the floor and top of the mosquito curtain were also black with it.

My month at Mannar went only too quickly and I decided to ride back to Jaffna all the way along the coast to Elephant Pass, a roadless journey with the sea on one side of one and the jungle on the other. Two or three evenings before starting, I sent for my horsekeeper in order to give him some instructions and the servants said that they could not find him. I had had my suspicions for some time that he was drinking, so I went out to the back to the stables and there I found him dead drunk. I have an intense dislike of drunkenness and almost a physical horror of drunken people, and in engaging servants I always told them that the one thing I would not tolerate was drunkenness and that they must clearly understand that, if they took the job, one condition of it was that if they ever got drunk, no matter where or when it was, I would instantly sack them on the spot. I had little doubt but that my horsekeeper had banked on the fact that there was not another horsekeeper in the whole Mannar District and that I could not carry out my threat. Next morning I sacked him, but found myself in a quandary. There was not a man in Mannar who had ever touched a horse or would have the courage to touch my horse. For a day or more the chief headman vainly tried to find me someone who would do so. But at the last moment a strange wild man of the jungle appeared and said that he would go with me to Jaffna as horsekeeper, though he had never had anything to do with a horse. He belonged to a small, remarkable caste of elephant hunters—the name, I rather think, was in Sinhalese Pannikkiya. They had a method of catching elephants handed down from time immemorial. Two of them went out into the jungle each carrying a strong rope. When they found a suitable elephant, they followed it, if necessary for days or weeks. They had to get it into such a position near a big tree as would enable them to creep up to it, slip a noose of the rope over one of his hind legs and tie the other end to the tree, which had to be strong enough to withstand the fury of the captured elephant. Eventually they had to contrive to get the other leg tied by another rope to another tree and I think they finally tamed him in the usual way by bringing up tame elephants who took him prisoner, as it were, between them. The Pannikkiya, who had spent a fairly long life in this precarious profession, was, I learnt without surprise and with relief, not afraid of my horse. He came with me to Jaffna, a taciturn man and not a very skilful horsekeeper, but a godsend under the circumstances. I had to arrange to return him safely to his jungle.

In Jaffna I acquired another horsekeeper, an admirable silent little man who remained with me until I left Ceylon in 1911. Sometime, I think it must have been in 1909, he came to me one day in Hambantota in a terrible state, saying that his wife was dying and that the Tamil doctors had given her medicine, but it did no good. Would I come and see her and give her English medicine? I went over to the room which they lived in by the stable and took her temperature. It seemed to me that she had a violent attack of malaria and I dosed her with quinine and covered her up with blankets. She recovered and their gratitude was extraordinary. He came to me soon after she had recovered and with great hesitation said that they knew that I was very fond of rice and curry, that the curries which the cooks made for English gentlemen were never really good curries because no men, only women, could make good curries—now he and his wife—for I had saved her life—were willing that she in future would always cook curries for me. She did and they were delicious curries.

When I got back to Jaffna in September, the routine of work and the Prices re-established itself, but my month in Mannar led to an incident which threw a strong light upon the hole in Price's psychology at the spot where, if he had had a heart, you would have found it. Though the whole thing concerned me intimately, completely fascinated, with a grim objectivity I watched him "dealing with" the situation. I think perhaps that I can best show what happened by quoting the account of it which I wrote to Lytton at the time:

March 24, 1907   Jaffna
I am sick and tired of things and I suppose I'm more than a fool for being so. I can look back and see myself astonished at my present state. You, I believe, when we meet will think of me as you and I used to speak of the vague, battered angels. It is only this that has put me out. By a series of accidents the Assistant Agency at Mannar became vacant. Government wired to the G.A. telling him to send me and actually appointed me to act as Assistant Agent. It was where I acted before for a month, but it is almost certain that this time I should have remained there. There are no white people there and it is nearly all jungle, but I should have liked it above everything. Besides it is practically unheard of for anyone to get a District after only $2\frac{1}{4}$ years out here. When the wire came, the G.A. was away. I could have gone at once, but knowing that he would not like me to go, I waited for his permission. I have described him to you: he has been very nice to me, but is a master of intrigue and has no heart at all. I foresaw the whole thing, but I seemed to be fascinated by wanting to see how he could contort and manage it. *He* wanted me above all things to stay here, because I do much more work for him than he could get most Office Assistants to do. But of course he could not "stand in the way of

my career". His line was that I was too young and that I should learn so much more by serving another year as Office Assistant. I was determined—partly because he had really been nice to me, I have almost lived in his house for a year—not to go without his full consent, but of course I checkmated that argument. I put him in such a position that I was practically bound to go or he would have practically to go back on his word. I went to bed on Thursday wondering how he would manage it but certain that he would prevent me going. He took his own way, quite wonderfully, for it showed that he had grasped my position absolutely. It would take too long to explain the minutiae of his method. But the end was that he wired to Government asking to be allowed to send Leak (the man who is theoretically my senior and superior here) instead of me *for the present* as it would be more convenient. What showed me that he had so completely grasped my position was that when he gave me the telegram he said: "of course if you prefer it I will tear this up now and you can go off tonight." At any rate the wire went and Leak is to go to Mannar. The position I had forced him into on Thursday was that he was to wire to Government asking to be allowed to send *no one* for a day or two, that he was to write to the Colonial Secretary and to say that if I was to get the place permanently he (Price) would not stand in my way, but if I was only going to act for a little time, he proposed to send Leak. Nothing more has been said of this arrangement. I never mentioned it again and I let him send his telegram because I was fascinated by watching his method. My whole object now is to force him to ask me the reason for my present coldness: but I think he is too wily. But he nearly from over-eagerness to justify himself gave himself away. When the wire of Government came approving his proposal, he asked me (damn him) whether I was pleased; the violence of my "No, not at all" absolutely threw him out and it was only his wife's coming into the room which saved him and, I suppose, me.

So I suppose I shall have another year in this accursed place.

I did not have another year in the "accursed place", for five months after I wrote this letter I was moved at a moment's notice to Kandy where Lewis was Government Agent; he had asked for me to be sent there as his Office Assistant. Price and I never mentioned Mannar again. I don't think I bore him ill will, for I had always known what he was like and it had even amused me to see him run so true to form. But I was glad to leave Jaffna and there is nothing more to say about my experience there except one curious incident which happened shortly before I left.

I have twice in my life had someone deliberately attempt to swindle me and both times escaped unswindled by the skin of my teeth. The first time was in the Jaffna kachcheri and I defeated the swindle by a deliberate forgery. One afternoon a Colombo Sinhalese sent his card in and asked me to see him. I cannot now remember what his business was, but it was something to do with the purchase of salt or it may have been land from the Government. I did not know anything about him and I was that afternoon extremely busy, but one was continually engaged in that kind of transaction and I had the clerk in and told him to put the thing through in the usual way. Some weeks later when the papers came up before me, I saw at once that the man in some complicated and ingenious way had tricked me into doing something which I ought not to have done and had thus deliberately swindled the Government. I could have taken a case against him, but it would have meant a long, tedious operation, and I suddenly saw that, with some slight risk, I could defeat him at his own game. It entailed either altering or destroying a document, but I was so infuriated that I did it. I then sent a letter asking the man to come up and see me. When he appeared, I told him that I had discovered his attempt to swindle the Government, but luckily he had forgotten or overlooked the snag (which I had deliberately created). I refused therefore to proceed with the transaction and told him that, if he thought he had a case against us, he must go to the Courts where I should be glad to meet him and reveal his business methods. I have never seen a man more astonished. I heard no more from him.

The other attempted swindle took place in Kandy and, if it had succeeded, it would have been entirely my own fault. I was sitting in the kachcheri late one afternoon holding a most exasperating enquiry—it was, I think, connected with a Kandyan divorce case. The Ratemahatmaya, the interpreter, the three parties to the case (the two husbands and wife), several witnesses were in the room in a circle round my table. The enquiry had dragged on all the afternoon, because the witnesses and indeed the principals came from some remote mountain village and were so overawed by the Kandy kachcheri that they became practically speechless and what they had to say had to be dragged out of them by me, the Ratemahatmaya, and the interpreter. As the day went on my room in the

Kandy kachcheri always became more and more hectic with an unending stream of people, clerks, peons, and headmen, bringing in documents and letters which required my signature or asking me to settle some difficulty. I was therefore always doing two or three things at the same time, concentrating in the centre of my mind on the main business—in this case the villagers and the enquiry—and attending on the periphery of my mind almost automatically with the routine stuff which the peons and clerks were continually putting on my table.

That afternoon a peon suddenly came into my room accompanying a white man whom I did not know. That immediately annoyed me. The longer I was in Ceylon, the more prejudiced I became against "white men". I had given a strict order to all in the kachcheri that, if a European wanted to see me, he was not to be brought into my room until he had sent in his card, explained his business, and I had said that I would see him. I did not mind much if a Sinhalese or Tamil wandered into my room and began pouring out his story—a not infrequent incident—partly because it made it more difficult for peons, clerks, and headmen to establish an effective barrier between the people and the O.A. or A.G.A. and exact exorbitant tips before a request or complaint could reach me. But I was infuriated when I saw a rather unpleasant looking white man introduced into my room by the peon without my permission. I let him stand in front of my table and went on with my enquiry as if he were invisible. Eventually I said to him: "What do you want?" "I want to get married", he said, "the day after tomorrow, and I have come to ask you, Sir, to issue a special licence." Among my other duties was that of Chief Registrar of the Province and special licences could only be issued from the Kandy kachcheri. I turned angrily upon the peon and said: "Why the devil do you bring the man here? Take him off to the registrar's room, tell Mr. Jayasuria to prepare the documents, and bring them to me for signature." Quarter of an hour later the man and the peon re-appeared and a sheaf of papers was laid on my table. I glanced through them and signed my name in various places and gave them back to the peon without looking at the white man or saying anything to him. They went out, but almost immediately afterwards the peon came back and, putting the papers in front of me and pointing to a place, said: "Master hasn't signed here." My enquiry had just reached a catastrophic climax and I was listening intently to the hesitating but crucial evidence in Sinhalese of a villager. I glanced at the paper which the peon had put before me, its image registering only on the periphery of my mind, and automatically signed my name. The peon went out and I returned to the enquiry, but three minutes later the image of the paper which I had signed jumped from the periphery of my mind to its centre and through the Sinhalese words of the witness I suddenly became conscious that, like an imbecile, I had been tricked and had endorsed a cheque. I shouted for the peon and told him to run after the man as fast as he could and bring him and the papers back, if necessary by force. A curious scene then took place. As soon as I looked at the man carefully, I saw that he was one of those louche but plausible international crooks who used to drift like the spores of some contagious disease from one Asiatic city to another. He had been reluctantly hauled back into my room by the peon and under my angry pressure he reluct-antly handed back the papers to me. I found as I had suspected, that he had obtained my endorsement to a cheque which would mean almost certainly that he would get his licence for nothing and ten or twenty pounds into the bargain. I tore his cheque up and told him that unless he paid for the licence in cash I would not give it to him. He tried to bluster, but I had him turned out of my room and out of the kachcheri. The clerks told me later that he had returned and paid in cash for the licence. The rest of his story I heard much later. He had somehow or other got himself engaged to the rather plain daughter of a respectable and fairly flourishing business man in Kandy. He bluffed his future father-in-law into providing him with the cash which he had so very nearly extracted from me. I cannot now remember whether he did or did not marry the unfortunate lady. At any rate almost immediately the bottom fell out of both her world and his. He had been swindling people up and down the country with dishonoured cheques, and warrants for his arrest were issued in Kandy, Nuwara Eliya, and Colombo. He bolted and managed to get on to a boat bound for Malaya. But in Malaya he was caught and sent back to Colombo where they tried him on many charges of obtaining money by false pretences and sent him to jail.

Chapter Three

KANDY

I TRAVELLED from Jaffna to Kandy to take up my new appointment on Monday, August 19th, 1907. It is a curious fact that I cannot remember anything about leaving Jaffna or arriving in Kandy or the journey, which must have taken a whole day, except two or three hours in the middle of it, and those two or three hours I remember after 53 years as vividly as if they had happened 53 minutes ago. I had to change trains at a station called, I think, Polgahawela and, as I had some time to wait, I went to the Rest House and lay in a long chair on the verandah. It was late evening and I was the only person in the Rest House. I had again on me that delicious feeling of setting out alone on a voyage into the unknown. The feeling was intensified by Polgahawela. What a soft liquid gentle Sinhalese word this—Field of Coconuts—was when one compared it with Tamil places like Kangesanturai and Kodikanam! And the place itself, the air, the trees, the sky itself were as different from those that I had left a few hours ago as the Sinhalese language from the Tamil. I had left behind me the bareness, austerity, burning dryness of the sands of Jaffna and now I was bathed, embraced by the soft, warm, damp, luscious luxuriance of the tropics. Here life was full of trees and changing leaves and, after the parched brown earth of Jaffna, it seemed to be embowered in ferns and flowers. As I lay back in my chair and looked up into the sky through the great trees, I saw through the branches the brilliant glittering stars, and all round the branches and the changing leaves were hundreds of tiny little brilliant glittering stars weaving a continually moving pattern—hundreds of fireflies. My two and a half years in Jaffna, the Prices, Gwen and the seaweedy sands on the shore, my bungalow on the wall of the Fort—all this seemed already to have faded away into a long-forgotten dream.

As soon as I got to Kandy, I found that I had indeed entered into an entirely new world. I am glad that I spent a year of my life at the age of 27 in Kandy, for life there was unlike any that I have ever known elsewhere, but I did not like it in the way that I liked Jaffna and Hambantota, and it did a good deal to complete my education as an anti-imperialist. Kandy was to a large extent Europeanized, it was a town of about 30,000 inhabitants, it was full of white men. There were far more Government servants, of course, than in Jaffna; there was a battalion of a Punjabi regiment with a Major Colquhoun and a subaltern whose name I have forgotten; there was a Gunner, a captain, a very nasty man, and an Army Pay officer, a major, one of the great Indian Lawrences, a very nice man; there was a white solicitor, a white manager of the bank, a white superintendent of Bogambra Prison, and white shop assistants. And all round on the hills and mountains right up to Nuwara Eliya were tea estates and white planters who were always in and out of Kandy. In addition—and this to me in many ways was very distasteful—there was always an air about Kandy of European cosmopolitanism and "society", for it was a beauty spot easily accessible from Colombo and its harbour, and so there was a perpetual stream of travellers, "passengers" as we always called them, to it, staying for anything from a night to a fortnight in the Queens Hotel down by the Lake.

There was a bungalow for the Office Assistant, a curious building up on a bank behind the great Temple of the Tooth, the Dalada Maligawa. It was a dark house, rather gloomy. For the first three months another civil servant lived with me, the Superintendent of Police, now Sir Francis Graeme Tyrrell. I do not like to share a bungalow or house, for the moment comes quite often when I want to be alone, and one of the unpleasant things about my first three years in Ceylon was that I almost always was living in someone else's bungalow or had someone else to live in mine. But of all the people I lived with out there, Tyrrell was far the best stable companion. He was very reserved, but very good company at the right time, unusually good-looking and with great personal charm. He was four years my senior and is one of the few of my Ceylon contemporaries who is still alive at the age of 84. When he went on leave, my sister Bella came out at the end of 1907 to stay with me. She was with me until I was transferred to Hambantota in August, 1908, and her presence made a great difference to my life in Kandy.

The work in Kandy was, as I have said, very strenuous. I used to get up at about 6.30 in the morning and have my early tea on the verandah. For physical enjoyment there are few things better than the delicious hour and a half after dawn in a semi-tropical place like Kandy. Everything in Kandy sparkles, including the air; it is wonderfully soft and cool before the sun gets up high overhead. About 7 a peon brought me four or five boxes containing all the letters. He opened them and I separated them out for the various departments, writing orders on them if necessary. In this way I was able to know exactly what had come into the office every day on the day. It was a pretty long business, but all the letters

were over in the kachcheri by the time it opened and I
went across to it. It meant that I worked without a break
from 7 to 12, when I returned to the bungalow for tiffin.
In the afternoon I worked in the office from 1 to 5 and
often later, and more often than not I had to work on
difficult papers after dinner in the bungalow. After the
office was the sacrament of tennis. Night after night we
all went up to the head of the Lake to the tennis courts, a
grander and more social ritual than that of Jaffna with a
continual flutter of females including a fluctuating stream
of visitors, planters, army officers, and their wives and
daughters.

After tennis I usually went down to the Kandy Club.
In those days in an Asiatic station where there was "the
Club", it was a symbol and centre of British imperialism
although perhaps we might not be fully conscious of
it. It had normally a curious air of slight depression, but
at the same time exclusiveness, superiority, isolation.
Only the "best people" and of course only white men
were members. At the same time there was none of the
physical luxuriousness, spaciousness, or at least comfort
of a London club; it was, indeed, a poky, gloomy, and
even rather sordid building. The habitués were the four
or five civil servants, Major Colquhoun, the Gunner
Captain, whose name I cannot remember, Lee, the
solicitor; every now and then, particularly at week-ends,
there would be an invasion of planters. The atmosphere
was terribly masculine and public school. Even if we were
not all gentlemen, we all had to behave, sober or drunk,
as if we were, although when some of us were drunk—
and drunkenness was not infrequent—it often seemed to
me a very curious form of gentlemanliness. The Club was
used for four purposes: to have a drink in, to play bridge,

to dine in, to play billiards. As far as I was concerned the purposes, when I went to it, were performed in that order. I went to it after tennis and had a drink and played a rubber or two of bridge. Sometimes I stayed and had dinner there, and, if I had not too much work waiting for me in my bungalow, played billiards or bridge again after dinner.

I can still feel what I felt the first evening that Tyrrell took me down to the Club. I was the new boy again, nervous and uncomfortable. Freud says in one of his books that civilization consists in the renunciation of instinctive desires and that the newcomer to a civilized society, the child born into it—the new boy in fact—has to learn again and for himself the renunciation. I am not naturally what is called a good mixer or a good clubman, and I have always felt acutely that what applies to the newcomer into a civilized society applies to me when I have to plunge into the (to me) icy waters of a circle of four or more strangers gathered intimately together. I have to learn all over again to adjust the mask of my words, the façade of my feelings, to the hail-fellow-well-met or the not-hail-fellow-well-met formula of the school cricket field, dinner in the college hall, or the Kandy Club. I was particularly ill at ease during the first weeks in Kandy. The narrow circle in Jaffna, in which after two and a half years there was nothing new for me to learn about anyone, had made me forget how to accommodate myself to a roomful of strangers. The consequence was that I immediately disgraced myself. It was at bridge, which was absurd, for I was quite a good bridge player, quite up to the standard of the Club. But I was set down to play a rubber with a cantankerous old judge, called Templer, the hard drinking, sardonic Major, and the

Chairman of the Ceylon Planters Association, Turner. I was the judge's partner, and I was terribly—and quite unnecessarily—nervous, and that was undoubtedly the explanation of why almost at once, holding quite a good hand which included six diamonds, I did not bid. When the hand had been played, "I suppose, Woolf", said the angry judge bitterly, "in Jaffna you don't bid diamonds unless you have thirteen of them." Inside I was as angry as the judge, both with myself and with him, and I was also miserable. It was a good example of how much deeper pain goes than pleasure, and unkindness than kindness, that I was not in the least consoled when, having played the very next hand extremely well, I was highly praised by Turner and even Colquhoun, and got a grudging acknowledgment from my partner.

In a week or two, of course, I had found my social feet in Kandyan society, bid diamonds when I had six of them, had readjusted my mask, façade, and carapace to my new environment, and so was accepted as a good fellow, a good bridge player, and a fairly good tennis player by most people—and even grudgingly by Judge Templer. Kandy was a terribly social place and after my sister came to stay with me, we were hardly ever alone, for she was an extremely sociable person, the kind of person who under the most unfavourable circumstances can help to "make the party go". Living in a kind of hill station, we were invaded socially from so many different sides. Apart from the large permanent circumambient population of planters, there was a continual coming and going of very important officials who, like the greater fleas, always bring in their train a number of less important officials. The Governor himself had a Residence, The King's Pavilion, and Sir Hugh Clifford, who for some time was

acting Governor, liked the place so much that he spent
a good deal of time there. He was a formidable man, but
by a piece of luck I happened to impress him as extremely
competent, and this not only had a considerable effect
upon my future career in Ceylon, but brought me into
direct contact with him and his exalted circle in Kandy
far more often than a mere Office Assistant to the Government Agent of the Central Province could have expected.

The most exalted region into which I stepped, partly
by an accident, but also partly with Clifford, was that of
an Empress, a real historical Empress or ex-Empress.
She was the Empress Eugénie of France. She was—
strangely, I think—a friend of Sir Thomas Lipton, who
made his fortune out of tea, and early in 1908 he lent her
his yacht to go round the world in. She arrived in
Ceylon in February, and, as she had been born in 1826,
she was then over 81 years old. One day in March a
telegram came from the Colonial Secretary to the G.A.
saying that Her Majesty the Empress would arrive the
following day in Kandy, that the Governor had lent her
the King's Pavilion where she would stay for a week, that
she must be met at the railway station on arrival, and that
everything should be done to make her visit a success.
The G.A. was, as usual, out of Kandy, so I put on my best
clothes and went down to the station to meet her. It was
an absurd ceremony and it was the only time in my life
that I have taken part as a protagonist in that kind of
royal reception. I took the stationmaster with me and two
or three policemen to see that no one got in the way of our
procession down the platform and I had arranged for a
carriage to take Her Majesty to King's Pavilion. When
the train stopped two ladies-in-waiting and two gentlemen-
in-waiting first got out of the carriage. I introduced my-

self to one of the gentlemen who told me that his name was Count Clary and he introduced me to the other three and to the Empress when she descended from the railway carriage. I told her that I represented the Government Agent and I hoped that she would let me know if there was anything at any time which we could do for her. The Empress seemed to me to be a tiny little bent old woman dressed completely in black with a black straw hat and a heavy black veil. I could not really see her face. The two ladies formed up one on each side of her and she began to walk slowly down the platform, while I, with the two gentlemen on either side of me, followed behind her. We crawled along at a snail's pace, stared at by a small crowd of spectators, and I was immediately given a lesson in the art of royal or diplomatic conversation by Count Clary. For no sooner had we begun to move than he looked up at the sky which was the bright blue, clear, cloudless sky of Kandy, and, in a tone of voice which was obviously calculated to put at his ease even an English official, said, "And do you often have thunderstorms here, Mr. Woolf?" By the time we had reached the end of the platform, he was telling me that his grandfather had spoken to a man who had been born in the 17th century.

The Empress must have assumed that I was in fact the G.A. and so the equivalent of a Préfet d'un Départment in France, for I received the following letter from Count Clary:

Wednesday, 4th March
King's Pavilion, Kandy.

My dear Mr. Woolf,

Her Majesty, the Empress, wants me to ask you to tea for tomorrow Thursday, at 4.30 p.m. If you have a previous engagement, just let me know, and it won't matter in the least, as Her Majesty would be sorry to disturb you.

Come in ordinary day-clothes.

Yrs very sincerely

Clary

On Thursday in ordinary day-clothes I went up to the Pavilion. The whole business seemed to me absurd, for the ceremonial was exactly what I imagine it would have been if the old lady, Eugénie-Marie de Montijo de Guzman, Comtesse de Téba, had still been the wife of Napoleon III and Impératrice des Français. The fact that she had ceased to be Empress of the French 37 years ago appeared to make no difference to the etiquette of her Court in King's Pavilion, Kandy. It seemed to me not inappropriate that the old lady in her make-believe Court should be, under a misapprehension, entertaining a young very pseudo-Government Agent. I was met by Count Clary with immense politeness and conducted by him into one of the smaller rooms—all rooms in King's Pavilion are very large—where once more I was introduced to the other three members of the retinue. After five minutes' fluent conversation one of the ladies-in-waiting left the room and returned immediately saying that the Empress would receive me. I was then led off by her and Count Clary to the enormous central room. Here a large square had been walled off, as it were, by screens and inside it a kind of throne room arranged with chairs and sofas. At the far end Her Majesty sat as upon a throne in solitary state. I felt vaguely that I ought to bow and kiss her hand, but that was beyond me, and instead we shook hands. A chair was put in front of her and I was invited to sit on it, while Clary and the lady-in-waiting stood on each side of the Empress. After a few minutes she rose and we moved in slow procession into another room where tea and the other gentleman- and lady-in-waiting awaited us.

We all sat round the table and the Empress talked or asked me questions. If you look her up in *Petit Larousse*, that monument of lexicography, all you are told about her is "Célèbre par sa beauté, elle eut une grande influence sur l'empereur, qu'elle poussa à défendre les intérêts catholiques dans le monde." Most women who have been so beautiful that their beauty (and often little else) is recorded in dictionaries and encyclopaedias—indeed also women of great beauty who have never been sufficiently famous or infamous to have their names recorded in *Petit Larousse*—when they are old or very old, retain in the shape of face or features or in the expression something from which you can see how beautiful they must have been. This was not true of the Empress Eugénie. In 1908 her face to me seemed positively ugly. Other accounts by people who knew her well do not agree with this; for instance, Ethel Smyth wrote of the Empress in *Impressions that Remained*: "I remember saying to the Duchesse de Mouchy that it was hard to believe that she could ever have been more beautiful than now, and the reply was: 'I think in some ways she is more beautiful now than when she was young, because years and sorrow have done away with the accidents of beauty—youth itself for instance, and colouring—and revealed the exquisiteness of design.'" Well, there you are—I may have been blind to all this, though I must say that what the Duchesse says about the "accidents" of beauty seems to me a little suspect—to call youth and colour accidents is to beg nine-tenths of the question.

The Empress was extremely affable, lively, talkative. Like nearly all great or very well-known people whom I have met, she asked innumerable questions and would not stay for an answer. All that I can remember of her conversation is that she made "curious thin little jokes" (as I wrote to Lytton), all of which I have naturally forgotten, and that she gave a very long, vivacious, but slightly silly, account of how when driving to the Peradeniya Gardens that morning she had seen a dog and a chicken fighting in the middle of the highroad. She was anxious to know whether dogs and chickens habitually fought in Ceylon, but when I said "No", I do not think she really stayed even for that answer. I was given a very regal, but warm, good-bye, and as I was making my final bow, Count Clary, with some assumed hesitation, said that, as I had been so good as to ask Her Majesty to let me know of anything which I could do for her, there was one thing Her Majesty would very much like to see, if that were in any way possible. Her Majesty had heard that the Buddha's tooth was sometimes shown to people and she had a great desire to see it; was there any possibility of my being able to arrange this? I said that I thought I might be able to arrange this for the afternoon of the day after tomorrow, and would let Count Clary know definitely later.

The facts about Buddha's tooth were strange. In 1908 in the great Dalada Maligawa, which means literally The Palace of the Tooth, but is always translated The Temple of the Tooth, there was housed one of the most sacred Buddhist relics, Buddha's Tooth. (The whole Maligawa was originally the King's Palace, the Temple, in Sinhalese vihare, being embedded in it.) In my day the relic was kept in a small locked inner shrine in the centre of the vihare; in the shrine was a table and on the table five bell-shaped caskets, called karanduas, one within the other like Chinese boxes, and under the last and smallest casket lay the Tooth. The Tooth could never be taken out or shown without the consent of both the Manager or Guardian of the Temple, the Diyawadana Nilame, in 1908 a fine old Kandyan chief and Ratemahatmaya, called Nugawela, and the Government Agent. In fact both the G.A. and the Diwa Nilame, as he was usually called, had a key to the shrine, and without the two being present the door could not be unlocked. In practice I, as O.A., kept the G.A.'s key, and arranged with Nugawela Ratemahatmaya for unlocking the door if and when the Tooth was to be shown.

The relic was shown annually at the great festival or Perahera every August, and otherwise only to very distinguished persons. In my year in Kandy I opened the shrine only three times, once for the Perahera, once at my request for the Empress, and once at the Diwa Nilame's request for Reginald Farrer, the Himalayan botanist, who had become a Buddhist. At the Perahera the Tooth was taken out of the Temple, placed on the back of an elephant and carried round the Temple in a procession before enormous crowds of Sinhalese who flocked into Kandy for the festival. If shown to distinguished persons, the caskets were taken off so that the visitor could see the Tooth, but it was not touched.

The reason for the institution of a joint guardianship of the relic by the Buddhists and the non-Buddhist Government was the disorder and ill-feeling which had arisen in the past and during the course of its unfortunate history. According to tradition, after being kept for 800 years in India, it was brought to Ceylon in the fourth century A.D.

About 1,000 years later the Indians of the Malabar coast captured it and took it back to India, but it was recovered and again brought to Ceylon by King Prakrama Bahu III in the 14th century. In the next two hundred years the island suffered from the chaos of lawlessness and war, and the Tooth was hidden in various places, including Gampola. There seems to be no doubt whatsoever that in 1560 it was discovered by the Portuguese, taken to Goa by Don Constantine de Braganza, and there publicly burnt by the Archbishop in the presence of the Viceroy of India. However a short time afterwards there were at least two "authentic" Buddha's Teeth in Ceylon. The present Tooth was established in the Maligawa by the Kandyan King in 1566 and it has remained there ever since. I have seen it, as I said, at close quarters three times and I should say that, whatever else it may be, it has never been a human tooth. If my memory is correct, it is a canine tooth, about three inches long and curved. Sir James Emerson Tennent, in his book *Ceylon* written in 1859, says: "Its popular acceptance, notwithstanding this anomalous shape, may probably be accounted for by the familiarity of the Kandyans, under their later kings, with the forms of some of the Hindu deities, amongst whom Vishnu and Kali are occasionally depicted with similarly projecting canines." But I think one can find a likeness to the Tooth nearer home than the Hindu deities; in my recollection its shape closely resembles that of the teeth of the Sinhalese Devils or Yakku who play such an important part in the everyday beliefs of the ordinary Buddhist Sinhalese and are always represented in their sculpture and mural paintings with projecting canine teeth curved upwards.

I got hold of the Diwa Nilame and he agreed to show

the Tooth to the Empress, and as Sir Hugh Clifford was
in Kandy, I told him about it for he had not seen the relic
and I felt sure he would like to be present. He met me outside the Maligawa and we waited in the road for the
Empress to arrive. When she came, an absurd procession
formed up. Clifford was a very tall man, over six foot high,
with a broad strong body and a large head and face. He
and the Empress led the procession and they walked so
slowly that it was like a slow motion picture, and the
Empress in the black clothes, black hat, and black veil of
the eternally black French widow was so short and bent
that Clifford could hardly get his head down low enough
to hear what she said through the thick veil. I followed
behind with the ladies- and gentlemen-in-waiting, making
the bright diplomatic synthetic conversation which is
appropriate when one walks officially in procession behind
an Empress of the French and the Colonial Secretary of a
British Crown Colony. It all passed off extremely well.
Nugawela, the Diwa Nilame, in full Ratemahatmaya
costume—you can see exactly what he looked like, for he
is sitting third seat from the left in the front row in the
photograph taken outside the Kandy kachcheri—was very
dignified and impressive and the Empress was suitably
impressed. I earned a good deal of unearned kudos from
the Colonial Secretary.

Despite the concentrated intensity and long hours of
my work in Kandy I lived a strenuous social life. For an
hour and a half every day I took violent exercise either at
tennis, squash rackets, or hockey. Rackets I played with
the Superintendent of Police, Alexander; he was a fine
figure of a man and an Oxford Blue and he was so much
better than I was that, although we must have played
dozens of games, I beat him only once and that must have

been by pure accident. I played hockey with the Punjabi regiment. They were absolutely mad on hockey and the subaltern asked me to come and play in their practice games whenever I liked to do so. It was a rather exacting business; they played like demons and some of them were very good, but they got frantically excited and, when they lost their tempers, dangerous.

There were three battalions in the regiment, one Moslem, one Hindu, and one, I think, mixed. Our men were Hindus and the two other battalions were in Colombo. Once a year they had an inter-battalion hockey tournament and the subaltern took our first team down to Colombo to play in it. The whole regiment was mad with excitement. For some reason the British officers never played in the tournament though subahdars did. Our team got into the final and in the second half they lost their tempers and the two sides went for one another with their hockey sticks. The officers, who were watching the game from the touchline, rushed into the mêlée to part the combatants, but before they could stop the fight two players had been laid out insensible.

I liked the Punjabis, but they could be curiously savage. On Saturdays we sometimes got up two scratch teams to play hockey; some planters, keen on hockey, used to come in to play; about six or seven men from the regiment, the subaltern, myself, and Lee, the solicitor, completed the 22 players. In one of these games I was much interested by what was obviously a "racial" incident. I was playing back, with a planter playing half-back on my wing in front of me, and he was obviously Eurasian, but not Ceylonese. One of our opponents, the outside-left forward facing us, was one of the best of the regimental players. For some reason, which seemed to me purely "racial", he took against the planter, and, whenever he got near him, instead of hitting the ball took a full-blooded swipe at the unfortunate planter's shins. I knew the Punjabi quite well and had often played with him, and I tried gently and tactfully to dissuade him from pursuing this vendetta. I was entirely unsuccessful and there followed a very painful scene. The planter, having received a crack on the shin for about the tenth time, lost his head, his nerve, and his temper; bursting into tears and shrieking wildly he went for his small, eel-like, elusive tormenter. We seized the two of them and the Punjabi was sent—smiling—off the field.

In writing an autobiography I find that every now and again I am in considerable doubt whether I ought or not to include some trivial or highly personal incident. Having been for 40 years both an editor who has to publish reviews by other people and a reviewer myself, I am very rarely surprised by what reviewers say. But I was slightly surprised (and much amused) to find that some reviewers of *Sowing*, the first volume of my autobiography, were irritated—almost outraged—by the fact that, though an intelligent man, I wrote quite simply about some incidents and my own reactions to them. For instance, the reviewer in the *Times Literary Supplement* said that he was "startled" because I remarked that "I remained a virgin until the age of twenty-five; the manner in which I lost my virginity in Jaffna, the Tamil town in the north of Ceylon, I will relate in a later chapter." The reviewer goes on to say: "Surely most people would find it natural to say either more or less about this event", and he complains that "again and again throughout the book the reader is given like occasions to wonder how such an intelligent man can claim to have such simple reactions." What amuses me in this is the writer's profound ignorance, not merely of my psychology, but of the way in which the mind and heart of all men, intelligent or unintelligent, work. Of course, many of the reactions of intelligent people are just as ridiculous, silly, and simple as those of the most unintelligent; the only difference is that in ordinary life we are clever enough to conceal the fact from the world in general and even from the not quite intelligent enough intellectuals. But if one has the temerity to write an autobiography, then one is under an obligation not to conceal. The only point in an autobiography is to give, as far as one can, in the most simple, clear, and truthful way, a picture, first of one's own personality and of the people whom one has known, and secondly of the society and age in which one lived. To do this entails revealing as simply as possible one's own simplicity, absurdity, trivialities, nastiness. Now it seems to me that almost any incident which has stuck in one's memory for fifty years—such as the hockey match which I have just described and one or two things which I am about to describe—are probably relevant either to the picture of the personality or to the portrait of the age.

The first incident was rather ridiculous. I woke up one morning feeling giddy and sick and, when I got out of bed, the room went round and round me and I had to sit down on the floor and crawl back into bed. I sent for a doctor and he, to my surprise, immediately diagnosed correctly the disease. He said that I had caught a cold in a nerve at the back of my neck and that if I stayed in bed for a day, I should be perfectly all right. For the next 24 hours I stayed in bed, doing my kachcheri work there, and as the giddiness had completely gone off, I got up next day and worked in the kachcheri. In the evening I

was due to dine with Mr. and Mrs. Middleton and their
rose-like daughter, Rose. He was a Judge of the Supreme
Court and was in Kandy holding the Assizes; he and Mrs.
Middleton were pleasant people, but almost impossibly
respectable. The Judge had rapped me on the knuckles
for not having attended his Court officially, as Deputy
Fiscal, at the opening of the Assizes. I had therefore to
be on my very best behaviour for the evening, which I
anticipated as pretty dull, though Rose was admittedly an
attraction. They were living in a house on the other side
of the Kandy Lake, which was perched perpendicularly
above the road and reached from the road by a flight of
25 or 30 stone steps. I went by ricksha and told the ricksha boy to come back for me about ten. The evening was
pretty dull and after dinner at about a quarter to ten, as
Mrs. Middleton was showing me some photographs, I
suddenly felt the appalling giddiness come upon me again.
Rather foolishly I thought that, if they saw me stagger
about, they would think I was drunk. So I said nothing
and held on grimly until ten, shook hands and by an act
of will and just holding on to chairs and tables got myself
fairly steadily out of the house and on to the terrace.
There I was faced by the terrifying flight of steps. I
managed somehow to get down upright half-way, but
then lost my footing and fell straight on to the ricksha,
to the amazement of the boy, who certainly thought I was
drunk. I managed to crawl into my own bungalow and
bed. Next morning when I woke up I was all right and
I have never again had a return of the disease.

The next Kandy incident is one of those curious affairs
of the heart which I find always fascinating and almost
tragic to observe, as they reveal the unending complica-
tions of the human mind and the human heart. I was very

friendly with a young man in Kandy, Christopher Smith. He came to me one day and asked me whether I knew the Misses Robinson. I only just knew them. They were the daughters of a planter, and Mrs. Robinson had taken a house in Kandy for a month or two and was living in it with her two daughters, Ethel aged 22 and Rachel aged 19. The two girls had a passion for riding and had brought their horses with them. Smith, who was 28, was extremely good-looking, intelligent, charming, but given to fits of moodiness, silence, and indecision. He told me that he was much attracted by Ethel and that almost every evening he rode with the two young ladies round the hills above Kandy. The difficulty for him was that he always had to take Rachel as well as Ethel and he therefore was never able to be alone with Ethel. Would I, like a good fellow, come and ride with them and contrive to be with Rachel so that he might have a duologue with Ethel? I must say that I didn't much fancy the job, but I liked Christopher—whom of course in those days I always called Smith just as he always called me Woolf—very much, and so I weakly agreed.

In 1907 Kandy and its surroundings were entrancingly beautiful. It was half-way between the low country and the high mountains and enjoyed the best of every climate and every world. The great lake, which was the centre of the European part of the town, lay in a hollow with the hills gently rising up all round it. These hills had been little built over and they were so covered with sub-tropical trees and flowering trees and flowers that the buildings were hardly visible. In the hills round and about the town a series of Drives and Rides have been constructed and named after the wives of Governors of Ceylon, Lady Horton's Walk, Lady Longden's Drive, and so on. They are extraordinarily romantic, winding in those days through unspoilt Kandyan mountain country with views of the Lake, of lovely Kandyan villages with their terraced paddy fields, of more distant mountain peaks, or the beautiful Dumbara valley.

Every evening for some weeks Smith and I used to ride with the two girls through these exquisite, gentle, flowery, deserted roads. I have said before that I do not know whether Kipling's stories were photographs of Anglo-Indian society and therefore of Ceylon society in 1907 or whether we modelled our lives upon the lives of Mrs. Hauksbee, Otis Yeere, and Mrs. Mallows. I remember sometimes in those rides with Rachel suddenly waking up, as it were, in the middle of Lady McCarthy's Drive or Lady Horton's Walk from a rather gentle, romantic dream, and asking myself whether I was indeed Office Assistant to the Government Agent, Central Province, who would have to go to the Bogambra Jail before breakfast next morning to see a man hanged, and who was now talking to a planter's daughter merely in order that Christopher Smith might talk to her sister, or whether in fact we were living a story by Kipling Under the Deodars.

I have always been greatly attracted by the undiluted female mind, as well as by the female body. And I mean the adjective "undiluted", for I am not thinking of the exceptional women with exceptional minds, like Cleopatra or Mrs. Carlyle or Jane Austen or Virginia Woolf; I am thinking of the "ordinary woman", undistinguished, often unintellectual and unintrospective. The minds of most women differ from the minds of most men in a way which I feel very distinctly, but which becomes rather indistinct when I try to describe it. Their minds seem to me to be gentler, more sensitive, more civilized. Even in the many stupid, vain, tiresome women this quality is often preserved below the exasperating surface. But it is not easy to catch it or bring it to the surface. You can only do so by listening to and by being really interested in what they say (and it is extraordinarily difficult ever to be interested in or listen to what anyone else, particularly a woman, says, because one is always more interested in and thinking about what one will say oneself after she has stopped talking).[1] I think I have taught myself gradually to be interested in what women say to me and to listen attentively to what they are saying, for in this way you get every now and again a glimpse or rather a breath of this pure, curiously female quality of mind. It is the result I suppose partly of their upbringing, which is usually so different from that of the male in all classes, and partly of fundamental, organic differences of sex. And that again I suppose is why, as a male, I get a romantic, even perhaps a sentimental, pleasure from feeling the quality.

It is necessary to say all this if I am to make clear to myself and therefore to my readers the nature of the relationship which developed in the long evening rides among the hills of Kandy between myself and Rachel. But first I had better deal with the protagonists, the *causa causans* of our rides, Christopher and Ethel. I became extremely uneasy about the whole business, because, as it

---

[1] Goethe shows in an amusing passage in *Elective Affinities* (quoted by H. O. Pappe in *John Stuart Mill and the Harriet Taylor Myth*) that he had noted this phenomenon: "Ottilie followed the conversation attentively though she took no part in it. The next morning Eduard said to Charlotte: 'She is a pleasant and interesting girl.' 'Interesting,' Charlotte replied with a smile, 'why she never said a word.' 'Did she not,' Eduard rejoined while he seemed to retrace his thoughts, 'how very strange!'"

seemed to me, Ethel was falling more and more in love with Christopher and he was completely unable to decide either to attach or detach himself. The situation was complicated by the fact that the moment was rapidly approaching when he was going back to England for six months. Nothing that I said could bring him to make a decision and eventually the day came for our last ride. He appeared in my bungalow in the morning and said that he could not face a last ride and that he had therefore sent round a message to say that he could not manage a ride, but would come round to the house in the late afternoon and say goodbye. He was not going to propose, and he besought me to come with him as he could not face a tête-à-tête with Ethel. I went and I do not think I have ever spent a more painful three-quarters of an hour.

As for Rachel, I liked her very much and reached the maximum of intimacy with her allowed by the extraordinary etiquette and reticencies of the age. It must be remembered that up to the end of our acquaintance she wrote to me as Mr. Woolf and I wrote to her as Miss Robinson. I had for her a real affection without ever at all falling in love with her; although she was not in the least intellectual and cared for few of the things for which I cared most, I liked the feel of her mind in the way I have described above, and so said to her what really came into my mind and listened, because I was interested in what she said. In the last letter she ever wrote to me, which was to tell me that she was engaged and would shortly marry, she reminded me—of what I had forgotten—that I had once given her a long dissertation upon matrimony and what her attitude to it should be. When I was transferred from Kandy to Hambantota, I did not see her for nearly two years, but then had a curious meeting with her.

I had been told by the Government to go up country and meet the Government Agent of the Province adjoining my District to discuss with him what new regulations we considered necessary for the control of rinderpest which was ravaging my District and his Province. I had a two-day journey by road and train right up into the central mountains in order to meet him, and the place of our meeting was quite close to Rachel's father's tea estate. Mrs. Robinson wrote and asked me to spend the two nights I would be up there on the estate. I accepted with alacrity.

I found it extremely pleasant to meet Rachel again and her mother and father were very nice to me. In the early morning before my meeting with the G.A. she lent me a fiery little chestnut horse and we went for a long ride. I had just spent a long time in the most solitary life in the dry heat of the low country and here suddenly I was galloping through the cool sparkling mountain air by the side of a young woman of whom I was fond. I had lived in Hambantota a life of complete chastity except for one curious night in Colombo when I had had to go there for my examination in Sinhalese. In all that time the only white women I ever spoke to were the wives of the irrigation engineers and that casually and rarely. I seemed now to be in a completely different world, the comfortable and comforting femininity of the Robinsons' bungalow —Mr. Robinson was an English country gentleman who had reconstructed his English environment on the top of a Ceylon mountain—compared with the austerity of my bungalow in the bare sandy compound down there in Hambantota.

My sister Bella, when she was staying with me in Kandy, had once gone up and spent a few days with

Rachel on this estate[1] and she had written to me that Mr. and Mrs. Robinson had spoken so warmly of me that she thought they would like me as a son-in-law. They were so nice to me now that I could not help rather uncomfortably remembering this. And before dinner on my last evening Rachel took me for a walk on the estate. We had slipped into a long silence and suddenly the narrow path turned round a great rock and brought us out on to a broad ledge with a sheer drop thousands of feet down to the sea level and the low country, and with a superb, terrific view over the miles and miles of jungle to, in the dim distance, the line of the sea and the coast—and somewhere there Hambantota and my bungalow. A strange, painful feeling came over me. I felt as if somehow I had been taken up into this high mountain and was being shown all the kingdoms of the earth and was being tempted, but the temptation was not the kingdom of the earth below, but in the girl beside me. I may be quite wrong about this, but I felt Rachel herself was waiting and I stood by her in miserable silence until we turned away and walked back silently to the house. In the house Mr. and Mrs. Robinson were waiting for us and I spent a very uncomfortable evening. I had a long journey before me next day, as I had decided to bicycle straight down the mountain side to my district instead of going half-way round the island through Colombo by train. So I had brought my bicycle with me to the estate and before dawn I got up and was given a cup of tea, and I said goodbye to Rachel. I saw her and her mother and

[1] In a letter to Bella when she was on the estate I made what I think is rather a good joke. I was keeping for Mrs. Lewis, the G.A.'s wife, while she was away from Kandy, her parrot. Unfortunately my cat killed and ate the parrot. I wrote the appalling news to Bella, adding: "Nothing can be done except to say: Requiescat in Pussy."

father only once or twice again, though she used occasionally to write to me even after she married. As dawn was breaking, I climbed by a rocky track to the top of the mountain, a coolie carrying my bag and bicycle, and then through the clouds and mist over the top and down on to a road. There I tipped the coolie, tied my bag to my bicycle, and coasted mile after mile down through the deliciously cool fresh mountain country until I reached the plain and jungles of the low country which from the ledge high up on the mountain last night I had looked down upon with Rachel by my side. At midday in the dry burning heat I came to the boundary of my District, and there waiting for me by the roadside was my horsekeeper with my horse and my dogs. I got on the horse and rode the weary miles to Wirawila and Tissamaharama in regret for Rachel, dejection, and yet at the same time with a kind of relief.

That, I suppose, was in 1909 or 1910; I must return to Kandy and 1907. There was too much work at Kandy, though I never really mind having too much work. Some of it I liked very much, but a good deal of it was boring or to me uninteresting. One was continually having to deal with the planters and their estates and labour, and there was much business connected with the sale and settlement of Crown Land. All this I found dull and irritating. On the other hand everything to do with the Sinhalese seemed to me enchanting. The Kandyans fifty years ago, both the Ratemahatmayas, the feudal chiefs and headmen, and the villagers were generally, and often also individually, the most charming people I have ever come across. They were typically mountain people, independent, fine mannered, lively, laughing, in their enchanting villages hidden away in the mountains, and isolated, unchanged and unchanging. It was extraordinary to deal with them after the rather dour Tamil of Jaffna living behind his cadjan fence under the remorseless sun in the unending plain. There was so much work in the kachcheri that I very rarely got out of Kandy itself for an enquiry in these remote villages, but the first time I did, I was astonished by my reception. I rode up 24 miles into the hills to a place called Urugala and arrived there after dark in a thunderstorm. Half a mile from the village the headmen and villagers met me in procession and brought me in with tom-toms and dancers. Then I had to stand in the rain for ten minutes while each member of the crowd came and prostrated himself, touching the ground with his forehead.

In a letter to Lytton describing this, I tried to defend the system, arguing that the Europeanizing of non-Europeans is a mistake, that it is best for every race to remain "as it was before Adam" (a curious and somewhat exaggerated idea). The Kandyan, I said, grovels on the ground and touches your boots, but has retained his independence and his manners. This letter reflects my growing awareness of the problem of imperialism and my personal relation to it in the plains of Jaffna, the mountain villages of Kandy, and later the jungles of Hambantota. For a long time I was uneasily ambivalent, exaggerating as in this letter, my imperialist, stern Sahib attitude to compensate for or soothe a kind of social conscience which began to condemn and dislike the whole system. Kandyan society in my day—quite apart from the O.A. to the G.A. Central Province, the G.A., the Governor and Government of Ceylon, and far off in London Edward VII by the Grace of God and the British Raj—quite apart from this extraordinary, hierarchical, and complicated engine of Empire and imperial government, Kandyan society in these villages was purely feudal. The Nugawelas, Ratwattes, and all the other great Kandyan landowning families were feudal chiefs, and the procession, and tom-toms, and prostrations which greeted the O.A. were merely an example of manners ordinarily displayed by the villager to the feudal chief, and now displayed towards the highly sophisticated product of St. Paul's School and Trinity College, Cambridge, who, by a cynical joke of history, represented Edward VII by the Grace of God in the village of Urugala on September 14th, 1907.

I do not think that anyone who has got close to a feudal society like this one in Urugala and all the other Kandyan villages, who to some extent has lived within it and has observed it passionately, sympathetically, and at the same time critically, can truthfully deny that on the surface it has socially a satisfying depth, harmony, beauty. And it was perhaps not only or entirely on the surface. I cannot believe that I was altogether mistaken and self-deluded when riding, walking, and talking to the smiling men and women in those villages. I felt that there was some depth of happiness rather than pleasure, of satisfaction, which is a good thing and which the western world is losing or has lost. Moreover, I was up above in the feudal hierarchy, one of the super-Chiefs, the Princes, or the Boyars, and, however much one may dislike the fuss and ceremony of social systems—and I do hate them —one cannot be impervious to the flattery of being a top dog liked by the underdogs. I certainly, all through my time in Ceylon, enjoyed my position and the flattery of being the great man and the father of the people. That was why, as time went on, I became more and more ambivalent, politically schizophrenic, an anti-imperialist who enjoyed the fleshpots of imperialism, loved the subject peoples and their way of life, and knew from the inside how evil the system was beneath the surface for ordinary men and women.

Another thing I liked about the Sinhalese was their religion. I am essentially and fundamentally irreligious, as I have explained in *Sowing*, but, if one must have a religion, Buddhism seems to me superior to all other religions. When I got to Kandy, I had already passed my examination in Tamil and I now had to take the Sinhalese examination. There is in the Maligawa a curious octagonal building, called the Oriental Library, because it contains some Pali texts; in my day the librarian was a Buddhist priest called Gunaratana. He became my pundit and taught me Sinhalese. Gradually I got to like him very much; we became friends and I used to go up into the Octagon of an evening when I could find time and sit with him on a kind of verandah overlooking the Lake and talk to him about Buddhism. It has to be admitted that he was the only real Buddhist whom I met in Ceylon, the only one who understood, believed, and practised the "higher" doctrines of this strange religion. As he explained it to me, it was a philosophy rather than a religion, a metaphysic which has eliminated God and gods, a code of conduct civilized, austere, springing ultimately from a profound pessimism. I could never myself believe in the Buddhism of this priest; it seems to me to be, like all metaphysics, a dream which is after all nothing but a dream. But it is a civilized and a humane dream of considerable beauty and it has eliminated most of the crude anthropomorphic and theological nonsense which encrusts other religions. There is another thing about Buddhism which appeals to me. I like the way in which every now and again a Buddhist will throw up his worldly life and withdraw into a life of solitude and contemplation. I know, of course, that these withdrawals are not unknown in other religions. But the Buddhist does not withdraw in order to do penance for his sins, to mortify or crucify himself or other people in order to obtain redemption, as others do. In the instances which I came across in Ceylon, he felt a sudden urge to leave the weariness, the fever, and the fret of his business and pleasures, his family, friends, and enemies, his loves and hates, and subside into solitude and simplicity. I once in Anuradhapura saw a man sweeping the courtyard round one of the dagobas. He was dressed like a sweeper, but there was something rather strange about him. I got into conversation with him and found that he had been a wealthy business man in Colombo; he was highly educated and spoke perfect English. Suddenly at the age of about fifty he had felt an irresistible desire to throw it all up and to follow the path of the Buddha which led him, not to penance or mortification of fakirs, saniyasis, dervishes, or monks, but to a life of gentle contemplation sweeping the courtyard of a dagoba. It is not a withdrawal and occupation which would ever appeal to me personally, but I respect the man to whom they appealed and the religion which inspired him.

There was much to be said against Buddhism and its priests fifty years ago in Ceylon. There were two establishments, both in Kandy, in which the Ceylon priesthood received its training, Malwatte and Asgiriya. My pundit, when he got to know me, talked frankly about things and he was, as a purist, greatly concerned at the maladministration and the corrupt teaching of Buddhism in the two establishments in those days. He had himself a very poor idea of the ordinary Buddhist priest turned out by them.

I often came across priests in the course of my official duties, and I must admit that my experience confirmed what he said. They were often very nice people, but their minds and their everyday life had as little connection with the Buddhism of the Buddha and my pundit as those of the ordinary village Rector in England have to do with the Christianity of Christ. The religion of the man in the street, the villager in the village, also had nothing to do with my pundit's religion, but Buddhism, perhaps wisely, accepts this and recognizes that different people must be given different beliefs, a different Buddhism, according to the stage of spiritual development attained by them. In practice, the result was that the religion of the vast mass of Sinhalese villagers consisted to a considerable extent of superstition and devil worship.

I shall always remember, as typical of this Buddhist flock and their Buddhist shepherd, a saffron-robed priest who came to my tent after I had had dinner one evening when I was on circuit in one of the remotest spots in my District of Hambantota, the roadless country in the foothills of the mountains of Sabaragamuwa. I gave him a chair and we sat together, first in the dusk and then the bright moonlight, outside the tent in a lovely meadow—so rare in that district—looking towards the graceful hills and beyond them the misty mountains. We talked and many villagers came and squatted round us near enough to take a respectful, but often amused, part in the conversation. The tranquillity and loveliness of this summer of the snakeless meadow—though I daresay the meadow swarmed with snakes—but that is what it felt like to me, so that when I looked across the meadow to the hills the tranquillity and loveliness brought a few sentimental tears into my eyes. But there was no sentimentality about my

Buddhist priest. He was a character, a card, a humorist, a realist. He flung himself about in his chair, cracked his jokes, violently rubbed his face and nose with his hand. He was priest of a small vihare in the neighbourhood, and all he thought about was its revenue, what he could get out of the land or the Government or anyone or anything on earth. He wanted to get something out of me—what it was I have completely forgotten. He talked and talked, and laughed, and watched me with his cunning beady eyes, and the villagers put in a word now and then, laughed respectfully when we laughed, and looked at one another, I noticed, occasionally out of the corner of their eyes. And I realized with amusement that he was not really a Buddhist priest; he was just like them, a villager, but in a saffron robe.

Yet, when all this has been said, Buddhism, even in its debased or most unsophisticated form, even in the devil-worshipping villager and his villager priest, was in many ways a good religion. The way of life as preached by Gautama Buddha is extraordinarily gentle, unaggressive, humane, far more so, it seems to me, in its verbal presentation and attitude than even that preached in the Sermon on the Mount. I think this gentleness and humanity somehow or other filters down even through the debased Buddhism into the minds and everyday lives of the most ignorant villagers. On poya days, the days of the full moon, I used to like to go and sit in the Maligawa in Kandy and watch the ceremony, the ceremony of a civilized religion. The villagers, whole families, men, women, and children, would flock in with their offerings of flowers. For hours the priest would sit reading from the sacred books, and all round him sat the people in family groups with their little children and babies, occasionally talking or eating, but imbibing unconsciously, it seemed to me, something of this doctrine of quietude and gentleness. It differed entirely from the scenes of worship in Roman Catholic countries, where people still flock into churches and cathedrals, for there was none of that horrible insistence upon sin and crucifixion, and much less tawdry worship of bad statues.

Since in the previous paragraph I have said something about Buddhism and Christianity as they appear to me, I ought to say something about Hinduism and Muhammadanism, both of which I have had to observe to some extent at close quarters. I had a good deal to do with Muhammadans and their religion for some time in Hambantota, as I shall explain later. From a purely practical point of view there is something to be said for this religion, just as there is for Judaism, to which it bears a family likeness. But it is too hard, formal, and hostile to the infidel to have any appeal to me. Hinduism, which was all about me for my two and a half years in Jaffna, is entirely different. In its ordinary, everyday form it repels me—the multiplicity of its florid Gods, their grotesque images, the ugly exuberance of the temples, the horrible juggernaut processions with the terrible retinue of fakirs, saniyasis, and beggars. All this prejudiced me against Hinduism and made me, I think, blind to some of its manifestations during my years in Ceylon. When I visited the island again after fifty years in 1960, on my way to Mannar I met in the Anuradhapura Rest House Sir Kanthiah Vaithianathan. When he heard that I was going on to Mannar, he asked me to come and see him at his house there and also the Hindu Tiruketheesvaram temple which he is restoring at great cost. He explained to me, as we went round, the symbolism behind the images and the ceremonies, and in his very clear and sincere exposition I got for the first time some idea of what "higher" Hinduism meant to a civilized man like my host. Like the esoteric Buddhism of my friend the priest Gunaratana, this esoteric Hinduism was a metaphysic rather than a religion. Yet it seemed to me inferior to Gunaratana's Buddhism, because it was a tiresome symbolism and therefore had never completely disentangled itself from the crude, uncivilized superstition connected with the Gods and Goddesses and their ceremonies.

To return to the Kandyan Sinhalese and my relations with them, as I have said, I was too much tied to my office in Kandy and only rarely could get away into their villages. But I got to know a good deal about them from enquiries which I had to hold in the kachcheri, and in particular from the strange procedure with regard to Kandyan marriages and divorce. This procedure was characteristic of the inveterate empiricism of British imperialism and British administration in Ceylon. The Kandyans have—or had in 1907—some very curious marriage customs or laws. There were two forms of marriage, *bina* in which the husband lived in his wife's house, and *diga* in which the wife lived in the husband's house. In certain cases polyandry was legal and customary, the woman being married to two brothers; the rights of each husband with regard to sleeping with the wife were strictly defined according to a timetable, for each had so many nights in a month. The British allowed these laws and customs to continue, but for some strange reason their administration was kept entirely in the hands of the Government Agent. That meant that in practice the marriage and divorce, in fact all the matrimonial affairs of these Kandyan villagers, were handed over to me, a young man who had been only two or three years in Ceylon. This fantastic system seemed to work quite well; at any rate the enquiries which I had to conduct in the kachcheri, particularly the divorce cases, fascinated me. From them I learnt a very great deal about the way of life of the villagers and the way their minds worked. Both the woman and the man had a right to a divorce on the ground of adultery, desertion, mutual consent, or inability to live happily together. It was the last ground which produced the most revealing cases, for they meant that one of the parties wanted and the other party did not agree to a divorce. Sometimes half the village might be called as witnesses and all the afternoon my room would be full of villagers. I am afraid that I must often have irritated my staff, headmen and clerks who had to be present, by allowing cases to drag on all the afternoon and witnesses to pour out their interminable stories, for if I encouraged them so that they forgot their fear and shyness in the strange atmosphere of my room, I would often get re-markable glimpses into the minds and domestic lives of people who, though on the surface so remote from myself, were to me fascinating, being often lovely to look at, charming, lively, gay, and sometimes tragic. Also it was extraordinarily interesting that every now and again you learnt in one of these cases what it was so rarely that you heard in Ceylon, the woman's side of the case. Not often, it is true, even in the Kandy kachcheri, but occasionally a woman bringing a case or resisting one would shed her genuine or assumed shyness and suddenly reveal in a torrent of words what her life, what her side of the picture was like up there in the mountains.

The most unpleasant work which I had to do in Kandy —and indeed everywhere in Ceylon—was connected with the prisons. The Government Agent held the office of Fiscal in his Province and the Office Assistant was Deputy Fiscal, and the powers and duties of the Fiscal were, I suppose, roughly those of the Sheriff in England. One of the Fiscal's duties was to be present in a prison when anyone was hanged or flogged and to certify that the sentence had been duly carried out. The G.A. or A.G.A. was expected to pay surprise visits occasionally to any prison in his territory and make a thorough inspection of it. No G.A. under whom I served was ever present at a flogging or hanging; he left that job to me. In Jaffna I had to be present when a man was flogged, and in Kandy I had to see six or seven men hanged.

The flogging of a man with a cat-o'-nine-tails is the most disgusting and barbarous thing I have ever seen—it is worse even than a hanging. The man is tied by his arms and legs to an iron triangle which is about six foot high and he is given the lashes by a warder in presence of the Deputy Fiscal, a Medical Officer, and the Superintendent of the Prison. His back is literally flayed by the lashes and every ten lashes he is examined by the Medical Officer who has to stop the flogging if in his opinion the man is not in a condition to stand any more punishment.

In Kandy executions took place in the Bogambra Prison in the early morning before breakfast. To be present at them was a horrifying experience, and the more I had to witness, the more horrible I found them—and I think this was the experience of almost everyone who had to be present. Kandy was, as I have already said more than once, a lovely place and it never looked more lovely than in the early morning when I stood in the Bogambra Prison in front of the gallows and everyone waited for me to give the signal to the executioner for the "drop" which would hang the man. I stood rather above the gallows, and in front of me in the fresh air and gentle sunshine just after dawn I looked across to the lovely hills surrounding the Lake. The procedure was that I first went to the condemned man's cell, read over to him the warrant of execution, and asked him whether he had anything to say. Some said no; several of them asked that their bodies after execution should be handed to their relatives; once the man said to me: "I have been guilty of a crime; I am glad to be punished." I think that all the men I saw hanged were Buddhists and were accompanied to the gallows by a priest. After I read the warrant, the condemned man was led out of the cell, clothed in white, on his head a curious white hat which at the last moment was drawn down to hide his face. In most cases they seemed to be quite unmoved as they walked to the scaffold, but one man was in a state of terror and collapse and had to be almost carried to the gallows by the warders, and all the way he kept repeating some words of a Sinhalese prayer, over and over again, and even as he stood with the rope round his neck waiting for the drop. The man was led up on to the scaffold by the warders, his arms were pinioned, and the hat drawn over his face. I had to stand immediately facing him on a kind of verandah where I could see the actual hanging. On the steps of the gallows the priest stood praying. In two out of the six or seven hangings which I had to certify something went wrong. In one case the man appeared not to die immediately; the body went on twitching violently and the executioner went and pulled on the legs. In the other case four men had to hang one morning and they were hanged two by two. The first two were hanged correctly, but either they gave one of the second two too big a drop or something else went wrong for his head was practically torn from his body and a great jet of blood spurted up three or four feet, covering the gallows and the priest praying on the steps.

I give these repulsive details because those who support capital punishment in the 20th century pretend that it is a necessary, humane, civilized form of punishment. As a form of punishment, it is disgusting and, as I saw it, disgustingly inefficient. From the point of view of society and criminology, in my opinion, it is completely useless. The men whom I saw executed had all committed unpremeditated crimes of violence, killing from passion, anger, or in a quarrel. Not one of them was deterred from killing by the fact that hundreds of other men in Ceylon had been hanged for precisely similar killings. All the evidence, in all countries and at all times, goes to show that capital punishment is not a deterrent of crime; in fact, by the mystique of horror which it creates it tends to induce pathological or weak-minded people to imitate the crimes for which men have recently been executed. This is particularly true today when uncivilized "popular" newspapers with gigantic circulations exploit —sensationalize and sentimentalize—the horrors, particularly of sexual murders of children, and a series of similar crimes follows. It is characteristic of these journals and their millionaire proprietors that they are hysterically in favour of retaining capital punishment as a deterrent while, by exploiting and sensationalizing rapes, murders, and hangings, they increase the number of murders and murderers (as well as their own incomes).

In Ceylon I saw for several years the working of the criminal law from the inside, in my small way, as administrator, as magistrate and judge, and as a public servant intimately concerned with the police and prisons. I have remarked in a previous chapter that I was never a lenient judge or magistrate. This was because I am convinced that it is absolutely essential that "law and order" should be strictly maintained, and that means that everyone knows what the law is and what are the penalties for breaking it. But that in turn means that the judge, whatever his private opinion may be about the goodness or badness of the existing law, must apply it to the man in the dock without fear or favour, impartially, justly, objectively, strictly, even sternly. In fact, I should say that the best chance of getting uncivilized laws abolished or changed is that they should be strictly applied by civilized judges who abhor them. Sitting on the bench or visiting the prisons in Jaffna, Kandy, or Tangalla fifty years ago, I felt again and again that much of our criminal law was both uncivilized and stupidly inefficient as a method of punishing or deterring crime. I am sure that it still is both in Ceylon and in Britain. In those days the prison system was more barbarous and iniquitous even than the law. The prisoners were confined in cages like those in the lion house in the Regent's Park Zoo, two, three, or even four men sometimes in a cage. The buildings were horrible. The prisoners hammered coconuts into coir or walked round and round the yard holding on to a moving rope which, I imagined, was a modern version of the ancient treadmill. I think the prison system has been considerably improved since those days. When I was in Jaffna in 1960 I met the Superintendent of the Jaffna Prison and he showed me over it. It was extraordinarily interesting to see it again after fifty years. There was no treadmill; the atmosphere of hopeless gloom and sordidness no longer existed; here at any rate was some small progress from barbarity to civilization.

GROWING

I was only a year in Kandy in the post of Office Assistant, for having arrived there in August, 1907, I left in August, 1908, to take up my duties as Assistant Government Agent, Hambantota, in the Southern Province. I had less than four years' service and this was extraordinarily rapid promotion, for I was the youngest A.G.A. and three years younger than the next youngest A.G.A. But it was not, I believe, my achievements in the everyday duties of an O.A. which won me this promotion; it was due to the Colonial Secretary, Sir Hugh Clifford, and I won his good opinion rather fortuitously. I think I first created a favourable impression on him by the way in which I dealt with the Empress Eugénie and Buddha's Tooth. The next episode clinched things. Clifford was a tremendous "lady's man", and while he was Acting Governor, a glamorous lady, the wife of an officer in the Indian Army, visited Kandy for a few weeks. One evening, riding with Rachel in Lady Horton's Walk, a carriage passed us in which sat Clifford and the lady, and even that brief glimpse showed that the lady had made a conquest of the Acting Governor of Ceylon. Some days later Clifford sent for me and asked me whether I could manage to arrange a first-class show of Kandyan dancing in the grounds of King's Pavilion. He would have a few friends dining with him the following Thursday and he would like after dinner to give them a first-class exhibition of this famous Kandyan dancing. He hoped that, if I could do this, I would come and dine with them and manage the thing afterwards for him, including the payment of the dancers. I said I could do this and I went to my old friend the Diwa Nilame, Nugawela Ratemahatmaya, and asked him to get the very finest show of Kandyan dancing ever seen in the Kandyan district. He really did so and it was superb.

He turned out all his retainers and headmen and an enormous company of dancers, tom-tom beaters, and musicians. He had about 100 torch-bearers and the dancing took place on the lawn in the light of the torches. The glamorous lady, for whom all this was done, was properly appreciative, and Clifford was immensely pleased. The only person slightly cynical about it was myself, and perhaps too Nugawela Ratemahatmaya. But I think it convinced Clifford that I was extraordinarily competent, and, when shortly afterwards an A.G.A. had to be appointed to Hambantota, on his own initiative—so he told me years later—he said that the post should be given to me. So on August 27th, 1908, I took the train from Kandy to Hambantota, reflecting that the fate, the whole life even, of an insignificant civil servant can be fortuitously determined by Empresses, the Buddha's Tooth, lovely ladies, amorous Governors, a few torches and dancers.

Chapter Four

HAMBANTOTA

I ARRIVED in Hambantota as Assistant Government Agent and "took over" from my predecessor on Friday, August 28th, 1908; I finally left it on leave for England on Saturday, May 20th, 1911. During my first years in Ceylon I had kept in close touch with the England and Cambridge which I had known, for Lytton and I wrote to each other continually. But gradually our letters thinned out and sometimes weeks or months passed without our writing. If two people are separated for years and by thousands of miles, they can write to each other either every week or only at long intervals. After two or three years I ceased to write to Lytton once a week, partly because I buried myself in my work and partly because I buried my past.

When I first came out to Ceylon, I was to some extent embittered and disappointed. My interests were passionately of the mind, though I was never, like Lytton and others of my friends, exclusively intellectual. I suppose that at the back of my mind, and in its depths, I wanted to be a writer. When I got to Ceylon, I found myself back at school. Nobody thought or talked of the things which I was passionately interested in. What I thought and felt about this I had to conceal from everyone in Jaffna and Kandy (except perhaps from Gwen on the seashore and Rachel in the mountains); my letters to Lytton were in part rage and lamentation, and in part a desperate effort to maintain contact. But after a time I seemed to harden

my heart against the past and against regret for the past.
I became almost fanatically interested in the country and
the people and in certain aspects of my work. I think that
my state of mind is honestly and accurately described in
the following letter which I wrote to Lytton about a
month after I arrived in Hambantota:

2nd Oct., 1908   Hambantota
                                         Ceylon

    I have often been on the point of writing in the last
months and never quite reached it, perhaps because I
knew that it would never be the time until you did.
Sometimes too I thought of that astonishing letter of
Ainsworth, do you remember it? the one I mean which
dropped on you after an interval of months dividing it
from the deluge of the previous delirium. And then
last mail I really thought you had written, a letter in
your handwriting with the Okehampton postmark and
when I opened it it turned out to be from someone
whose whole letter was about hunting on Dartmoor and
returning to Ceylon. And by the same post came a
postcard with Hunter's Inn on it. God, it seemed all so
old. And before I had quite recovered from it, the next
day when no mail should have come your letter came.

    The scene had changed here too and one changes
inside too. After all I am today and to be impinged
upon by innumerable todays, the change is inevitable.
I have no connection with yesterday: I do not recognize
it nor myself of it. I am of and in today moulded and
marked by innumerable things which have never
touched you and when I come back and find you all the
same, someone will say quite truly as Moore once said
of Sanger or Crompton or someone who had almost

reached the twilight: "Really they seem to be interested in none of these things."

And I suppose I am happy too, happier I expect as far as quantity goes than you. I work, God, how I work. I have reduced it to a method and exalted it to a mania. In Kandy I worked about ten hours a day and played in tennis tournaments and went to intolerably dull dinners and duller dances and played bridge and drank and became the bosom friend of planters. So as a reward a month ago they sent me here as Assistant Government Agent. A "reward" because it is what they call "a charge", I am on my own in my district which is about 1000 sq. miles with 100,000 people in it and I am supposed to be very "young" to have got it. So I live at the Residency Hambantota. There are no Europeans in Hambantota itself[1] . . . 26 miles away on one side are two Europeans a judge and a Supt. of Police and 20 miles away on the other is another an Irrigation Engineer. There is also another Irrigation Engineer who suffers from chronic indigestion and fever 20 miles away in the jungle I don't quite know where. But the house, really it is worth coming to Ceylon to live in it. It must originally have been built by the Dutch with walls of astonishing thickness and an enormously broad verandah and vast high rooms. It stands on a promontory right away from the town and right over the sea. Day and night you hear the sea thundering away almost at the gates of the compound, which is vast with nothing in it but sand and three stunted trees and is surrounded by a wall which the

[1] This is not quite accurate; there was a Belgian missionary, Father Cooreman, who had a Sinhalese school. He was a very nice man, but I rarely saw him.

wind which blows here unceasingly has blown into
ruins.

The District of Hambantota which was now committed
to my charge lay in the extreme south of Ceylon. Bounded
on the south by the sea, it was about 100 miles in length;
its breadth was never more than 30 and in places was
only about 10 miles. Except in the north-west it was
entirely flat; it lay in the dry zone, the low country. It
had three divisions: Magampattu in the east, East Giruwa
Pattu in the centre, and West Giruwa Pattu in the west.
Magampattu was almost entirely covered with jungle. It
contained the small town of Hambantota, but otherwise
only small scattered and usually poverty stricken villages.
Twenty miles east of Hambantota was Tissamaharama
with a major irrigation work and a resident white
Irrigation Engineer. Here was a great stretch of
paddy fields irrigated from the tank and a considerable
population of cultivators. Besides producing rice at Tissa,
Magampattu also produced salt. All along the coast eastwards from Hambantota were great lagoons or lewayas.
In the dry season between the south-west and the north-
east monsoons the salt water in these lewayas evaporates
and "natural" salt forms, sometimes over acres of the mud
and sand. Salt in my day was a government monopoly,
and it was my duty to arrange for the collecting, transport, storing, and selling of the salt—a large-scale complicated industry. Magampattu was also famous for its
game and wild animals. In the extreme east there was a
Government Game Sanctuary of about 130 square miles
in which no shooting was allowed; I had a Game Sanctuary
Ranger and some Watchers to look after it. There was a
small area to the west of the Sanctuary in which only

resident sportsmen might shoot. The issuing of licences
to shoot big game—elephant, buffalo, and deer—was in
my hands and in the open season sportsmen from all over
the world used to come to Hambantota for big game
shooting. I got to know a great deal about these sportsmen
and the business of big game shooting; the more I learned,
the less grew my love and respect for those who shoot and
for those who organize the shooting.

West of Magampattu, separated by a fair-sized river,
the Walawe Ganga, lies East Giruwa Pattu and then West
Giruwa Pattu. Here the scenery changes completely. The
jungle disappears; there is more water, more rainfall; it is
quite populous with prosperous villages, with rice and dry
grain and coconuts. In the north-west corner, where the
foothills of the mountains begin, the country is as lovely
as anything in the Kandy district. Yet it was Magampattu
and the eastern part of the district which really won my
heart and which I still see when I hear the word Hambantota: the sea perpetually thundering on the long shore,
the enormous empty lagoons, behind the lagoons the
enormous stretch of jungle, and behind the jungle far
away in the north the long purple line of the great mountains, from which I looked down that evening with
Rachel.

One's memory in connection with places is curiously
erratic. There are two things about my house in Hambantota which I remember vividly. If you walked towards the
sea across the compound, you came out upon a hillock of
fine white sand, which was the tip of the promontory. To
the right was an absolutely straight stretch of about two
miles of the sea shore, dazzling white sand. All the year
round day and night, if you looked down that long two-
mile line of sea and sand, you would see, unless it was very

rough, continually at regular intervals a wave, not very high but unbroken two miles long, lift itself up very slowly, wearily, poise itself for a moment in sudden complete silence, and then fall with a great thud upon the sand. That moment of complete silence followed by the great thud, the thunder of the wave upon the shore, became part of the rhythm of my life. It was the last thing I heard as I fell asleep at night, the first thing I heard when I woke in the morning—the moment of silence, the heavy thud; the moment of silence, the heavy thud—the rhythm of the sea, the rhythm of Hambantota.

The second memory is of sight, not sound. In the early morning when I was having my early tea upon the verandah, regularly every day at exactly the same hour a long line of about 30 or 40 flamingos flew over the sea along the two-mile stretch of coast from west to east. When they came to the headland upon which the Residency stood, they made a right-angle turn to the left and flew inland immediately over my house to the great lagoon which lay to the north of the town. It was a lovely sight and every morning I used to go out into the compound and watch the marvellous manoeuvre. The birds flew in perfect formation single file, and as they flew along over the sea the line was gleaming black and white. Then as each bird in turn wheeled to the left high up in the air above the house, it suddenly changed in the bright sunshine from black and white to a brilliant flash of pink.

During my years in Hambantota I lived a life of intense solitude. It was a social solitude—I had no social life. In the day, of course, except when I was on circuit in the jungles of Magampattu, I was surrounded with people and continually talking to people. But that was my work; the people were Sinhalese talking Sinhalese. They did not come to my house nor did I go to theirs. When I went on circuit to Tangalla, 26 miles to the west, the largest town in my District, I found Southorn, the District Judge, and Hodson, the Superintendent of Police, and we dined together. When I went on circuit 20 miles east to Tissamaharama, I found Wilson, the Irrigation Engineer, and we would dine together. But such meetings were, at the most, once in a month. Occasionally the head of a department or some high official would come to my District on official business and he would stay the night with me. Twice in my three years I had to entertain the Governor on an official visit of some days. During the open shooting season, there was always a trickle of European "sportsmen" into and out of the District, Princes, Counts, Barons, and less exalted people, soldiers, planters. All of these people I had to deal with in one way or another. Otherwise I never saw a European and I had no social life at all. I worked all day and after dinner I worked or read. I learned in Hambantota to like solitude and I do not think I ever felt what people call loneliness.

In my letter to Lytton I said that I had exalted my work to a mania. This was quite true. After three years in Ceylon I had put out of my mind and out of my life, almost deliberately, everything which until I left England I had considered most important. I immersed myself in, I became obsessed by my work—but only with one side of my work. I disliked the European side of it, the white sahib side of it, the kind of second-rate (as it appeared to me) pomp and circumstance which surrounded one in Kandy and Colombo. I am deep down within myself an extremely ambitious person, desiring success. At the same time I despise success and those who pursue it, even to some extent those who attain it. It is usually much less

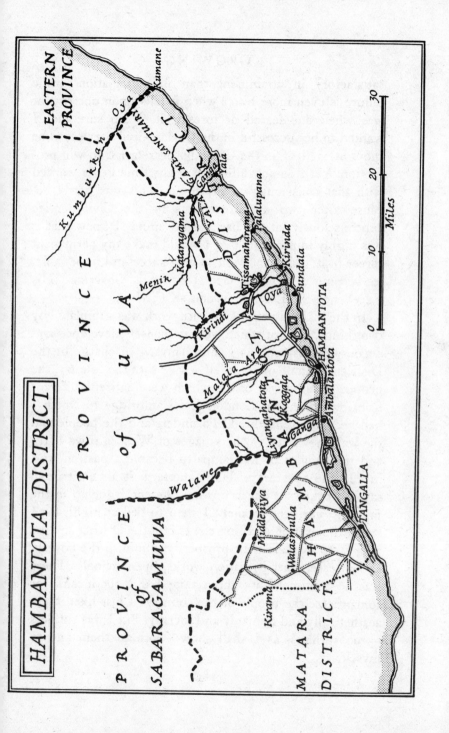

satisfactory in attainment than in anticipation, while failure is even more bitter when it falls upon one than it was when one feared or foresaw it. I am sure that I wanted to be successful in the Ceylon Civil Service, to be thought well of in the Colombo Secretariat, to win promotion. Yet I do not think that at any time I ever worked with that consciously in my mind. This was partly because after two or three years in the Civil Service subconsciously, at the back of my mind, I knew that it was highly improbable that I would make my permanent career in it. I did not want to be a successful imperialist, to become a Colonial Secretary or a Governor, His Excellency Sir Leonard Woolf, K.C.M.G.

In the main my obsession with work was stimulated by two things, both of which were immensely developed and encouraged as soon as I found myself in charge of the District of Hambantota. I fell in love with the country, the people, and the way of life which were entirely different from everything in London and Cambridge to which I had been born and bred. To understand the people and the way they lived in the villages of West Giruwa Pattu and the jungles of Magampattu became a passion with me. In the $2\frac{3}{4}$ years in Hambantota, it is almost true to say, I worked all day from the moment I got up in the morning until the moment I went to bed at night, for I rarely thought of anything else except the District and the people, to increase their prosperity, diminish the poverty and disease, start irrigation works, open schools. There was no sentimentality about this; I did not idealize or romanticize the people or the country; I just liked them aesthetically and humanly and socially. But I was ruthless —too ruthless, as I shall show—both to them and to myself.

The second impulse which determined my mania for work was a passion for efficiency. I think I have always had this dangerous passion. If I have to do something, I almost always immediately get a consuming desire to find out "the best way to do it", the most economical, quickest, most efficient, the most methodical. This desire is theoretically admirable and its results are often admirable; but it is very dangerous for it tends to become a ruthless obsession so that one forgets that efficiency is a means to an end, not an end in itself. My promotion to Assistant Government Agent enormously encouraged this desire for efficiency. Suddenly I found myself on my own, responsible for a vast variety of administrative operations, and my experience had already shown me that administration was almost always and everywhere slow, unintelligent, badly organized. I set out to make the Hambantota District the best administered in the island, and I do not think that I deceive or flatter myself when I say that I succeeded. I will give an example or two which will, I think, prove this and will also show the kind of life which I had to lead and the kind of work that an "imperialist" administrator performed in a British Crown Colony fifty years ago.

The first example concerned an operation which was not routine or part of the everyday administration. In my last year I had to take a Census of the District. It had to be done through the village headmen and the organization was extremely difficult. Nearly the whole population was illiterate and the enumerators were not much better in many places. For days and days I went round and round the District personally instructing the enumerators, held a "preliminary" census, and checked every enumerator's schedules filled up at this preliminary census. There was always a good deal of competition among the A.G.A.'s to see who could get his District returns in first. Mine was a difficult District because in many places there were long distances between the scattered villages and no roads. But the Mudaliyars (Chief Headmen) and their subordinate headmen had learned in the last two years my passion for efficiency and intolerance of inefficiency. The enumerators had been drilled so that they really knew how to fill in the forms. The Census night was March 10th, 1911. I organized a system of bicycle relays to get the returns in promptly. It worked so well and the messenger was so eager that he woke me up at 4.30 a.m. to give me the West Giruwa Pattu returns. On March 11th and 12th, the Mudaliyar of Magampattu, the Head Clerk of the kachcheri, and eight other clerks sat with me from 7.30 a.m. to 7 p.m. each day checking returns. On March 13th I wired the figures to the Superintendent of Census in Colombo and he replied that they were the first District returns to be received by him. The final figures, showing an increase during the past decade of only 5,617 or 5·3 per cent, which was less than I had expected, were:

Magampattu	11,799
East Giruwa Pattu	12,948
West Giruwa Pattu	85,740
Total	110,487

As A.G.A. I was responsible, as I have said, for the Government salt industry. As soon as salt formed in a lewaya, I had to arrange, through the Salt Superintendent and the Chief Headmen, for its collection. The collectors had to be recruited from the villages and they often had to come considerable distances. This required careful timing and organization, for unless the salt was promptly collected a shower of rain might destroy it or it might go wrong and turn into epsom salts. After collection I had to arrange for the transport of the salt from the lewaya to the Government salt stores at Hambantota or Kirinda. After tenders had been called for, this was done on contract at so much per ton by contractors in Hambantota who owned, controlled, and hired bullock carts. We sold the salt from the stores either to the Hambantota contractors and carters who transported it in the bullock carts, right up the long straight north road down which I had bicycled from Rachel's tea estate, and sold it up country to traders and planters, or to a large Colombo firm, Delmege Forsyth & Co., for transport by sea to Galle and Colombo.

Some little time after I arrived as A.G.A., when I called for tenders for the removal of salt from the lewayas, it was clear that the contractors were forming a ring with a view to forcing me to pay 20 or 30 cents a ton more than before. I felt that their idea was that here they had a much younger and less experienced A.G.A. to deal with and that I would yield to pressure. For a time I refused to give a contract at all and hired carts direct from the carters. Up to a point this was eminently successful, but it was a slow laborious business and the contractors knew that it could not go on indefinitely. So they tried a new dodge. They offered to remove salt from a distant lewaya at Rs. 1·70 per ton. Then suddenly they all stopped work and left the lewaya and put a pistol at my head saying that they would not remove the salt at less than Rs. 2 per ton. In my official diary I record that

In the evening I got hold of the previous contractor and I was determined that he should take another contract. Eventually with great difficulty and a certain amount of pressure I induced him to enter into a contract to remove 10,000 cwts. a month until all the salt on this side of the lewaya is removed. As he will probably pay the carters about Rs. 1·50 a ton, I feel that I have scored. He undertakes with me to do it at Rs. 1·80 per ton, which is the old rate.

In the diary I discreetly do not specify how exactly I applied "a certain amount of pressure". It was rather unconventional. The Salt Superintendent brought the contractor to me to the kachcheri where I was working late in the afternoon after everyone else had left. I tried unsuccessfully every possible means to induce him to take a contract at Rs. 1·80 per ton; he stood out for Rs. 2. At last I said to him: "I have been sitting here working since 9 o'clock this morning and I want some exercise and fresh air. I am going for a walk on the Tissamaharama road. There is, of course, no need for you to come, but I shall be very glad if you will, so that we may go on discussing whether you agree to Rs. 1·80." He was, I think, rather pleased to be asked to go for a walk with the A.G.A. and the Salt Superintendent, and he would be seen by all his friends and enemies walking with us through the town. We discussed the matter as we walked in the usual squirrel cage of fruitless argument. When I got to the first milestone on the Tissa road I stopped and said: "Now, Abdul Rahman, will you take Rs. 1·80?" and when he shook his head, I said: "I am going to walk on to Tissa and I should like to go on discussing the matter with you, but don't come, if you don't want to." He felt, I think, that it would be rather awkward or rude to turn back by himself and so we set out for the second milestone. The

Tissa road is very straight and bare through scrub jungle
and by the side of the lagoon; it seems to take a long time
to walk a mile on it. The evening was warm and fine; the
world about us was completely empty except for the
darkening sky above our heads and the unending road
beneath our feet. Abdul Rahman was not a good walker
and the Salt Superintendent, a large Malay, showed signs
of wilting. At the second milestone I stopped and said:
"Now, Abdul Rahman, will you take Rs. 1·80?" and when
he shook his head, I said: "I am going to walk on to
Tissa which, if we go on at this pace, we shall reach about
two in the morning, for we have another 18 miles to go.
I am very fond of walking and I think the Salt Superintendent is too. But I don't want you to come on if you
would rather not." Off we set again, but after a bit,
Abdul Rahman stopped; he looked at the Salt Superintendent and shook his head; then he turned to me with
a smile: "Well, Your Honour, I'll take the Rs. 1·80."
We walked back, my companions limping slightly, but
the best of friends. The tale of Abdul Rahman and
his Rs. 1·80 became a legend in the District in various
versions, and I never had any more difficulties with the
contractors.

In several ways I revolutionized the salt industry in
Hambantota. I completely altered the system of paying
the collectors so that they were paid on the spot. Hitherto
they were given payment vouchers which could only be
cashed in the Hambantota kachcheri, a system which led
to a regular trade in vouchers by middlemen who bought
them at a considerable discount from the collectors. This
made it much easier to get labour for the collecting, and
it was largely owing to this that the amount of salt collected in 1910 beat all previous records. We collected and

stored 224,352 cwt. The largest total collection pre-
viously was 189,563 cwt. in 1893.

When collection was going on, I often suddenly got on
my horse and rode ten or twenty miles to pay a surprise
visit. No one knew when this severe A.G.A. might not
appear riding on the horizon and discover someone not
doing his work or taking an illicit commission on the sly.
One day I became suspicious or received a hint that a
certain amount of hanky-panky was going on over the
removal of the salt from the lewayas into the Government
stores. The salt was bagged and weighed at the lewaya
and the weight of salt marked on the outside of each bag
just before transportation. They were weighed again on
receipt at the store and the weights recorded. Between
receipt at the store and sale a certain maximum amount of
wastage was allowed; it followed that if the weight of salt
in a bag was marked as less than in fact it was and so
recorded as received in the store, a pleasant little primrose
path was opened for dishonesty. So one afternoon I suddenly appeared in the Hambantota stores when I knew
that they were receiving salt from a lewaya. A cart had
just arrived and I checked the weight of each of its bags.
I found that there was an excess of 36 lb. over the weight
given at the lewaya. I tried another cart of 18 bags and
found an excess of 15 lb. I then found that in practically
every case in which I had not been present, the weight of
a cartload, according to the checkers at the stores, had
been *less* than the weight as given at the lewaya.

It was clear from this that the weighing at the lewaya,
for which the head guard was responsible, and the weighing at the store, for which the checkers were responsible,
were both inaccurate and in every case the recorded
weight was less than the actual weight, the inaccuracy

therefore being on the side which would show the least wastage when a store was emptied. By this time the Salt Superintendent had arrived on the scene and I told him that the checkers and the head guard must be suspended for six months from all Government service. The checkers pleaded that it was unfair to rely on figures obtained by checking only two carts. I agreed to go on checking carts, on condition that an additional six months' suspension would be given for every cart which confirmed my deduction. Looking back it seems to me that there were unnecessary severity and relentlessness in this decision. The checkers foolishly agreed and we weighed another cart. The weight recorded on the bags was 51 lb. less than the actual weight.

My third example concerns a terrible catastrophe which fell upon my District early in 1909. An outbreak of rinderpest had occurred in the island and there were cases of the disease in the Uva Province which adjoined my District. On February 18th there were three cases of the disease among bulls in Hambantota town. These bulls had been transporting salt in carts to the tea estates in the Uva Province and had become infected there. They had been turned loose with another 250 head of cattle out on the Maha Lewaya adjoining the town. I had the sick bulls isolated and rode down to the lewaya in the evening, had all the cattle there rounded up and counted; I put them in charge of watchers and ordered them to see that none were removed and no other cattle brought to the lewaya.

This began a struggle against catastrophe which lasted for a whole year. I never worked as hard or as despairingly and relentlessly as I did during those twelve months trying to stop the spread of the disease and to save some of the people's cattle. Rinderpest is a terrible disease and to see an outbreak of it in a place like the Hambantota District is horrifying. It is extremely infectious and, if introduced into a herd, practically every animal caught it and the mortality rate was very high. It attacked all cattle including the buffaloes. It is a cruel and disgusting disease; often I have come upon a diseased bull or buffalo wandering about in a field or jungle with half its face eaten away by maggots. The only possible way of stopping or controlling the outbreak was to insist upon (1) the immediate isolation of any infected animal and all contacts, (2) the continual tethering or impounding of uninfected cattle. The difficulty of doing this was tremendous. There were no fences or hedges and all cattle were allowed habitually to wander about everywhere. In open places near towns or villages, like the lewayas, you would always see herds of two or three hundred cattle. In Magampattu one had to think not only of the domestic cattle and buffaloes, but also of the large numbers of wild buffalo which soon became infected and spread the disease to the tame buffaloes.

Cattle and buffalo were the people's most valuable property; the prosperity of the whole district depended upon them. It was almost entirely an agricultural district and rice, the most important crop, was dependent for ploughing and threshing upon cattle and buffaloes. Everywhere the only form of transport was the bullock cart, and in Hambantota town, as I have already said, there were a large number of carters, many of them Muhammadans, who depended for a living upon the transport of salt, and so upon their bulls who pulled the carts. As the disease spread, the Government made regulations that all cattle should be tethered or impounded, and that all infected or stray cattle should be destroyed.

For months I spent hours and days trying to control the disease and limit the disaster, riding hundreds of miles in order to try to enforce the regulations and shooting stray cattle and buffaloes on the roads and in villages as a warning. The kind of thing which I did is shown by the following extract from my official diary for June 26th, 1909:

I have received several complaints from the G.A. Sabaragamuwa that rinderpest is being spread from East Giruwa Pattu into Sabaragamuwa at Kachchigala. This is a most inaccessible place but as the Mudaliyar of East Giruwa Pattu who has been removed from service has not been able to effect anything I decided to make a forced march up there. I bicycled early in the morning to Mamadola 14 miles where my pony met me. From there rode to Wetiya on the Liyangahatota road (5 miles). Here were two bulls suffering from rinderpest in a gala. Struck across country to Abesekaragama (3 miles) where "the Abeskera of Abesekaragama" (an old dismissed Vidana Arachchi of the old type with any amount of influence) met me and showed me all his cattle enclosed in the paddy fields. Then on to Metigatwela wewa (about 3 miles) where I found a very different state of affairs, buffaloes straying about round the tank. I shot two, one of which was diseased, the whole of one eye and part of one side of the face had been eaten away by maggots but the wretched beast was still straying about. I got some rice at Metigatwela and then rode on to Uswewa (2 miles) and Kachchigala (1½ miles). Here I found no stray and no diseased cattle but after enquiry I found that the headmen have undoubtedly been remiss. I am going to punish them and prosecute the chief offender. From Kachchigala there is a path to Kandaketiya ($1\frac{1}{2}$ miles) and from there to Talawa (4 miles) which I reached about 7.30 p.m.

Next morning at Talawa a villager told me a curious story about buffaloes. I had several times during the outbreak been told that buffaloes which got the disease would often break out madly and travel long distances to die in the place where they had been born. According to this Talawa villager the disease had been brought to the village in the following way. Four years before a man in Talawa sold a she-buffalo to a man at Alutwewa, a village about 8 miles away. For four years this buffalo never came back to Talawa. But, he said, a week or so ago she got the disease at Alutwewa, broke out of the pattiya "as if she were mad", and was found the following morning lying dead in the fold at Talawa in which she had been born.

These forced marches in a desperate attempt to save something from the disaster were not only exhausting— for riding and enquiring for $12\frac{1}{2}$ hours with only "some rice" at Metigatwela under the Hambantota sun is a pretty strenuous day—it was also terribly depressing. I remember one day in particular when in the evening I felt acutely the failure and futility of what I was doing. I had spent the whole day driving and riding round a heavily infected area, destroying animals and warning owners wherever I found stray cattle that I should have to destroy them if I found them straying again. Late in the evening I drove through a small village which I had already visited in the morning. By the side of the road I came on two cows straying, one already showing symptoms of disease. I sent for the owner and he proved to be a man whom I had warned earlier in the day. I felt that I must, as one said, make an example, and I took my rifle from my trap and shot the two animals. It is not a pleasant business to ride and drive through villages and shoot the cattle and buffaloes of the villagers whom one knows and likes.

The whole village seemed to have turned out and the men were standing on the road round the bodies of the animals; there was a hostile murmur from the small crowd. I explained to them that the owner had been warned, that by not impounding his animals he was infecting them and helping to spread the disease to other people's cattle all over the country. As I walked to my trap, they followed me and, as I drove away, I still heard the dull hostile murmur of their voices.

It was the only time in my three years in the Hambantota District, in my seven years in Ceylon, that I heard that note of communal hostility against myself or the Government from villagers (though I did hear it once from a crowd of carters in Hambantota). It is a very disturbing sound. I was profoundly depressed. I knew that the order to impound cattle was practically futile, because it would not be obeyed and could not be enforced. I knew that the villagers did not believe what I said to them; to them I was part of the white man's machine, which they did not understand. I stood to them in the relation of God to his victims: I was issuing from on high orders to their village which seemed to them arbitrary and resulted in the shooting of their cows. I drove away in dejection, for I have no more desire to be God than one of his victims.

I spent the night in a tent or circuit bungalow—I forget which—not many miles from the village, and I had

arranged to meet there the Muhandiram or chief headman of the area to discuss with him these rinderpest difficulties and problems. The Muhandiram was a very
intelligent Sinhalese, English educated; he had been sent
to Hambantota from another district where he had held a
higher post—in fact he had been demoted for some error
or offence. I liked him and talked quite freely to him as I
would have to a white man. He came to me after I had
eaten my dinner and we strolled out to a headland discussing the administrative problem of enforcing the
rinderpest regulations. When we came to the end of the
headland, we looked eastwards from a low sandy cliff over
the sea. It was the days of Halley's comet. The head of the
comet was just above the horizon, the tail flamed up the
sky until the end of it was almost above our heads. The
stars blazed with the brilliance which they have only on a
clear, still, black night in the southern hemisphere. And
at our feet the comet and the stars blazed reflected in the
smooth, velvety, black sea.

We stood in silence; it was a superb spectacle; as a
work of art, magnificent. And I suppose it was what is
called awe-inspiring. But there is something about these
spectacular displays of nature, about the heavenly bodies
and the majestic firmament which, while I admire them
as works of art, also irritates me. From my point of view
—the human point of view—there is something ridiculous about the universe—these absurd comets racing
round the sun and the absurd suns flaming away at impossible speeds through illimitable empty space. Such
futility is sinister in its silliness. I turned to the Muhandiram and asked him what he thought about the comet
and the planets and the stars. His answer depressed me
even more profoundly than the Sinhalese villagers. He

believed quite seriously in all the astrological nonsense
which the *Daily Express* supplies to its white readers
today. Our lives and characters, he said, were determined by the position of the constellations at the
moment of our birth. I foolishly tried to convince him of
the absurdity of such an idea. I might just as usefully have
tried to prove to the President of the Royal Society that
the earth is flat and the sun goes round it. He told me that
at a female child's birth the horoscope predicted the year,
day, and hour at which her menstruation would begin, and
it was always accurate. If I would tell him the place and
hour of my birth, he would have my horoscope drawn
and it would prove to me that my life and character had
been determined by the position of the heavenly bodies at
the time of my birth.

The incidents of those twenty-four hours in the rinderpest ravaged district of Hambantota were no doubt
trivial, but they could be read as a moral tale about imperialism—the absurdity of a people of one civilization
and mode of life trying to impose its rule upon an entirely
different civilization and mode of life. As I stood with the
Muhandiram looking at the great comet blazing in the sky
and in the sea, I was ruminating on this moral tale and
it was the cause of my dejection. For my attitude to
the Hambantota villagers was entirely benevolent and
altruistic; I was merely trying to save from destruction
some of the most valuable of their few possessions.
Following me and murmuring as I walked to the trap
they had less understanding of my ways, my intentions,
my affection for them than the half-bred bitch walking at
my heels. They were the nicest of people and I was very
fond of them, but they would have thrown stones at me
or shot me in the back as I walked to the trap, had they

dared. And the Muhandiram, through whom I was attempting to impose our rule upon them, so quick-witted, so intelligent, so anglicized and Europeanized—scratch the surface of his mind and you found that he believed that Halley's comet, the blazing constellations above our heads, the planets in their courses, the spiral nebulae, the infinite galaxies flaming away into space, had been created and kept going through billions of billions of years in order that a grubby little man in the Hambantota bazaar could calculate the exact day and hour at which the Muhandiram's infant daughter would have her first menstrual period.[1]

The destruction and devastation caused by the disease were terrible. Less than a year after the outbreak began I went to the Game Sanctuary and rode through it to see the effect there. The disease had died out among the wild buffaloes, but immense numbers had died. I recorded that "I have not seen 25 buffaloes, though I went about to look for them, where last year I must have seen two or three hundred." Among the village cattle, the herds roaming on the lewayas, the cart bulls, the valuable tame buffaloes used in large numbers for agricultural purposes under the great irrigation works, like Tissa, and in rice cultivation under village tanks, the mortality was appalling.

The sights which one saw continually filled one with despair. For instance, I was driving to Tissamaharama from Hambantota one afternoon, during the height of the outbreak, to stay the night there and hold some enquiries, when I was stopped near Wirawila, where the road passes through thick jungle, by a headman, a Vidana Arachchi.

[1] Of course, one must admit that he may be right, and that that is the object of the universe.

I knew him well, a gnarled little man who had some knowledge of the jungle. There was a well-known water hole about $1\frac{1}{2}$ miles through the jungle on the left of the road, and he told me that it was in a terrible state as there were bodies of dead buffaloes in and around it. It was the dry season and there would be no water for miles round except in this water hole. The Arachchi asked me to come and have a look at it. It would be the night of the full moon, so I told him that I would and that I would spend my night at the water hole. I was very fond of sitting up over a water hole in this way and just watching the animals come and drink; I took my rifle and sent my horse-keeper with the trap to Wirawila, telling him to come back and pick me up at six the next morning.

It was a fantastic night. The scene round the hole was indeed terrible: in the water hole itself were the carcasses of four wild buffaloes and a sambhur; round the rock were four dead wild buffaloes and two dead pigs. At first I did not think that I could stand a night there. But I wanted to see whether animals would come to drink and what would happen. Walking round the hole I came upon the body of a wild pig, obviously partly eaten by a leopard. The Arachchi agreed with me that the leopard would probably return to it at dusk and he asked me to shoot it as leopards were causing destruction among the village cattle who had so far escaped the disease. We piled up some branches on the ground about three or four yards from the carcass—the ground was very awkward and that was the best we could do. We lay on the ground behind the branches and I rested my loaded rifle on them. The light began to fade and a mongoose appeared, and disappeared into the belly of the pig. A leopard is the quickest and most silent of all jungle creatures. I was looking the whole time intently at the carcass and then suddenly with no warning, without my seeing a movement of his approach, there was the leopard standing upright a few yards from me, staring straight into my eyes. I looked straight into his eyes, fascinated, so fascinated by his ferocious eyes and his magnificent beauty that I could not shoot, did not think of shooting. The Arachchi made a tiny movement to attract my attention, for he thought I did not see the leopard. At the same moment there was a sudden violent scuttle of the terrified mongoose out of the pig. The next moment there was no leopard there; I did not see a movement of his departure any more than I had seen a movement of his arrival. It was as though some colossal hand had wiped him instantaneously out of the picture or the world. The Arachchi shook his head; he obviously thought I was either cracked or afraid; if I had had time to think, I should certainly have been terrified, but in fact in this instance I had been so entranced by the beauty of the creature that there was no time for fear.

We walked back to the water hole and on the way I saw a most extraordinary sight. It was now bright moonlight and about 100 yards off down an opening in the jungle was a jackal. He was entirely alone, performing what seemed to be an intricate dance. I have twice in my life seen March hares in the Sussex water-meadows performing their extraordinary dances. The jackal seemed to be doing the same thing. Leaping into the air, almost turning somersaults, silently and all by himself, after the mongoose and the leopard's cold eyes staring into mine, he seemed to be part of a completely silent, slightly mad, sinister world.

It was a wonderful place for watching animals come to drink at night. The water hole itself, long and narrow, was

in the middle of a great square plateau of solid rock, about
400 to 500 yards each way. It was surrounded on all sides
by thick jungle and was raised above the jungle so that
the tops of the nearest trees were level with it. On one side
of the water hole and about 5 or 6 yards from it rose
a great rock or gigantic boulder, 12 or 15 feet high
and quite smooth and flat on the top. One could lie on it
all night and get a fine view of the water hole and, raised
up there, of an immense sea of trees and changing leaves,
stretching away below one, beneath the light of the moon,
into infinity and eternity.

The wind had dropped; the moon was so bright that I
could have read small print in its light. After the ferocious
heat of the day the freshness of the midnight air was
delicious. Watching at a water hole like this is enthralling.
As the night goes on the silence of the jungle grows
deeper and deeper, but every now and again it is broken
by a soft, sibilant shiver of all the leaves of all the trees for
miles round one. This colossal whisper dies away as suddenly as it floats up out of the trees—complete silence to be
broken again by strange snufflings and shufflings of some
invisible creature nearby, the rattling of a porcupine's
quills, the sudden snarl far off of a thwarted leopard, the
bell-like call of a deer, or the tortured howling of jackals.

That night for several hours nothing came out on to the
rock to drink until, between two and three in the morning,
a great crashing and cracking began down there in the
jungle and slowly drew nearer and nearer to the rock.
Then an immense head appeared out of the trees in the
moonlight and an elephant shouldered himself up on to
the rocks. He was followed by another and another and
another until there were ten elephants lined up along the
water hole. The old bull stood at one end of the line and

down at the other end were two or three tiny calves standing between their mothers' forefeet. The whole line waited for a few minutes, each beast swaying, fidgeting, lifting up one foot after another in that pattern of eternal restlessness from which no elephant for a single moment seems able to escape. The whole line swayed and fidgeted and flapped their ears, but the only sound was the slight shuffling of their feet upon the rock. At length, the bull put his trunk towards the water, but he did not drink— it was too foul to drink; he stood still for a moment, flapping his ears, and then, raising his trunk and trumpeting, he turned away from the water hole and lumbered off. Orderly, one after another, keeping the line in single file, the other elephants followed the bull.

After that I fell asleep. I have always found it difficult to keep awake all night at a water hole. Though one is lying or sitting on hard, bare rock, one is overcome with sleep, and, though I have often woken up soaked with dew and stiff in every joint, I have never slept more profoundly or dreamlessly. That night I was terribly hungry because I had intended to dine at Tissamaharama and the only food which I had had since midday was two or three biscuits. But I slept like a log until I was woken up by the sun again on my face. As I walked the $1\frac{1}{2}$ miles through the jungle to the road, two magnificent elephants broke through the trees one on each side of me, making off towards the distant river. They too must have visited the water hole and found the water undrinkable.

It was extremely difficult to get any idea of whether or not the enormous amount which we did for a year or more to combat the disease and save some of their cattle for the cultivators had any effect. What filled me with despair was that as soon as I thought that at last we had got to the end of the outbreak, the disease would start up again in some God-forsaken spot and the horrible business would begin all over again. I thought at the time that we had succeeded to some extent in saving cattle in the populated parts of West Giruwa Pattu. In the jungle-surrounded arable areas of Magampattu, like Tissamaharama, where tame buffaloes were being continually infected by diseased wild buffaloes, I did something by large-scale removal of uninfected buffaloes to remote places where they might escape infection. For instance, I removed 450 buffaloes from Tissa to three different places, and 283 survived the outbreak. If they had remained at Tissa, I do not think that 30 would have survived.

The loss of practically all the cattle under the great Tissa Irrigation Work was a terrible disaster. The people did not plough their paddy fields; the usual method of preparing the fields for sowing was what is called "mudding", i.e. buffaloes are driven round and round the wet fields until the soil is properly stirred up. By the middle of 1909 there were so few cattle left alive that it became clear that unless something was done, there would be practically no cultivation of rice in the autumn. I got from Colombo some light English and American ploughs and some Agricultural Society instructors to give demonstrations. The struggle against the conservatism of the cultivators was extremely interesting. At first they would not look at the ploughs; "Hamadoru," they would say to me, sorrowfully shaking their heads, "no bull could pull that plough; you would want an elephant!" However we persisted. One of the difficulties was to get bulls and train them; I got the Mudaliyars to obtain some bulls and took them down to the Hambantota lewaya in order to train them and myself to plough. It was literally ploughing the sand, and amused not only me, but the inhabitants of Hambantota town. Then I took the ploughs and bulls to Tissa and gave demonstrations there. Almost at once I got applications for 80 or 90 ploughs, which I immediately ordered from Colombo. In the end 3,140 acres were cultivated, of which 2,420 were ploughed, 570 mudded, and 150 worked with mamoties. The yield of the ploughed fields was considerably higher than the others, but to turn buffaloes into a paddy field and drive them round and round was much less trouble for the cultivator than ploughing with a badly trained bull, and after I left the District I believe that everyone gave up using the English ploughs.

The Hambantota District used to be called a "sportsman's paradise". There was a great deal of "big game" in the jungles of Magampattu: leopard, bear, elephant, buffalo, sambhur deer, spotted deer, and pig. Both in Magampattu and in the two western pattus snipe were plentiful in the wet season, and on the lewayas and irrigation tanks there was good teal shooting. Before I came to the District I had done very little shooting, but I soon began to do quite a lot of it. The food which one got normally in a place like Hambantota was very dreary, particularly the eternal aged stringy curried chicken. Apart from sport, therefore, one shot for the pot: deer, jungle fowl, peafowl, teal, pigeons, snipe, golden plover. I had the extraordinary luck to win in a sweepstake two years running: £17 in the Colombo Turf Club Grand National sweepstake, and then at the end of 1908 on a Rs. 10 ticket £690 in the Calcutta Turf Club Melbourne Cup sweepstake. I spent some of this money in fitting myself out with gun and rifles.

I am a terribly bad shot with a rifle and not a good shot with a gun. But, like almost everyone from the Tolstoys of the world downwards, shooting and hunting at first fascinated me. The excitement is tremendous, whether you are stalking a deer in the jungle, shooting snipe in a paddy field, or waiting in the evening on a tank for the sound of the whistling of the teal as they fly in to roost on the dead trees and give you the chance of a shot at them as they circle high over your head. I always remained a very poor shot, but I got to know the ways of the jungle and of its birds and beasts quite well so that I was a fairly good tracker. But, like many other sportsmen, the more I shot the more I came to dislike the killing. In my last year I spent as much time as I could afford in the jungle, observing the animals and sitting up at night over water holes, but I gave up shooting except for food.

I had under me a Game Sanctuary Ranger and Game Watchers to look after the Game Sanctuary and also generally the shooting and protection of game outside the Sanctuary. The Game Sanctuary Ranger was a strange man. His name was Engelbrecht, a Boer from the Orange Free State. A considerable number of Boers who fought and were captured in the Boer War were sent to Ceylon and were interned in camps up country. Engelbrecht was one of them. When the war was over, the prisoners-of-war were repatriated to South Africa on condition that they took the oath of allegiance to the king and his successors. Engelbrecht was the only one of them who refused to take the oath, on the not illogical ground that he knew who the king was and what he was like, but he knew nothing about his successors. Nothing would move him, for he was, as I found, one of the most obstinate men in the world (and also a very stupid man). So the Government sent him down to Hambantota on a miserable allowance to live in a disused prison, the idea being that he would find life so hard and dreary that he would give in. But the Boers are a stiff-necked race and Engelbrecht was a Boer of the Boers. One of my predecessors who was A.G.A. Hambantota in 1906 reported to the Government that Engelbrecht was living in the greatest poverty and squalor and something ought to be done about him, and he recommended that the Boer should be appointed Game Sanctuary Ranger on a small salary. The Government agreed.

Engelbrecht was a first-class shot, a good tracker and shikari, and he soon learned a great deal about the Ceylon jungle and its ways; he taught me three-quarters of what eventually I learned about shooting and tracking. He was a cold-blooded man, the only man whom I have known who seemed to me to be completely without fear and without nerves—I saw him, as I shall tell, perform in cold blood an act of incredible bravery and foolhardiness. He was tall, straight, and very thin, his hair and beard reddish, his eyes small, very light blue with a glint in them every now and then of icy malignancy. He behaved to the Sinhalese as the Boers behave to the Negroes in Africa and, not unnaturally, he was hated in Hambantota. This led to some nasty incidents.

Being Police Magistrate as well as A.G.A. I used to walk over from the kachcheri to the Police Court to try cases in the afternoon when I was in Hambantota town. One afternoon when I got to the Court I found half the male population of the town packed into the Court, on the verandah, and all round the building. There was one woman, a good-looking Sinhalese carrying a baby. There was obviously going to be a *cause célèbre*, and I was rather surprised that neither anyone in the kachcheri nor the Court Interpreter had warned me of it. We began with the usual string of nuisance and similar cases in which the

accused always pleaded guilty and was fined a few rupees.
Then the woman's case was called and the defendant
pushed his way through the crowd of spectators and came
and stood below the bench. The defendant was Engelbrecht. It was a paternity case by the woman against him.
He denied paternity. There was, however, very good
evidence that he had been living with the woman in the
old prison, and she unwrapped the naked baby and held
it up to show me that it was a white baby. It was extremely
interesting to watch the faces of the men packed in and
around the Court. There was none of the usual stir and
movement, no smiles, lifting of eyebrows, shakings of the
head. They stood quite still, expectant, their eyes fixed
first on the woman, then on Engelbrecht, then on me. I
knew them well enough by now to know exactly what was
passing through their heads. "He is a white man, this
swine. The A.G.A. doesn't really know what he's like; he
goes out into the jungle and shoots with him. What will
the A.G.A. do?" I found for the plaintiff and made a
maintenance order. There was no sound from the crowd;
their faces remained impassive, rather grim; but there was
a distinct drop in tensions, a kind of soundless sigh of
relief as they filed out of the Court.

I do not think that Engelbrecht ever mended his ways,
and the people revenged themselves upon him twice in a
horrible and cruel way. He travelled, of course, always by
bullock cart when on circuit in the jungles and Game
Sanctuary. He had two magnificent cart bulls—I do not
think I have ever seen a finer pair of bulls. One morning
he woke up to find the bleeding heads of his two bulls
placed one on each side of his doorstep. After enquiry, I
had little doubt that the people who had done this were
the brothers of the woman who had borne him the child.

But the people of Hambantota saw to it that there was no evidence which could possibly have led to a conviction.

The second case was even more unpleasant. One day Engelbrecht shot a she-bear and then found a small bear cub in the grass nearby. He took the cub and reared it. He had a small Sinhalese boy who drove his bullock cart and the bear became passionately devoted to the boy. I have never known a more charming animal than this bear. He was half-grown when I first knew him, and, when I was on circuit in the jungle or Game Sanctuary with Engelbrecht, he would follow us all day like a dog along the tracks, only stopping to dig out an ants' nest if he came upon one. He slept with the boy on a mattress under the cart, and when I was travelling with them, the last thing at night I always went to have a look at the pair fast asleep under the cart with their arms round each other's necks. One day when Engelbrecht was out in the jungle on circuit, the boy got a thorn in his foot which became badly poisoned so that Engelbrecht had to return at once to Hambantota. When he got to his lodging in the prison, he shut the bear in and carried the boy up to the hospital. The bear somehow or other managed to get the door opened and started off snuffing along on the scent of Engelbrecht's boots up the road to the hospital. Everyone in the town knew the bear and knew that it was harmless; but they also knew that it was Engelbrecht's, so some of them beat it to death in the street.

Engelbrecht's act of fearless foolhardiness took place just after dawn one morning in the Magampattu jungle. The Assistant Superintendent of Police at Tangalla was a young civil servant called Hodson. He had never been in the jungle proper and had done no big game shooting. He very much wanted to begin, so when I had to go on a short circuit to the Game Sanctuary, I took him with me. On the way back we camped one night near some great rocks which had caves in them. Just after dawn next morning, we went out with Engelbrecht in order to give Hodson a chance to shoot a deer or possibly a bear or leopard. We were walking slowly in single file, Hodson in front with his rifle, near the rocks when a leopard crossed our path about 25 yards ahead. Hodson fired and hit the beast for we found and followed a trail of blood right up to the rocks and into a cave. The cave had a large entrance about 12 foot long by 20 foot high, but at least half the entrance was blocked by an enormous rock or boulder about 6 foot long and 6 foot high. The rock itself sloped sharply up to the actual lip of the cave so that, as we three stood peering into the darkness, we could rest our elbows and therefore our rifles on the floor of the cave. A wounded leopard is one of the most dangerous of all animals, and to follow him into a dark cave is sheer madness, as Engelbrecht knew even better than I. At first one could see nothing in the cave, but when our eyes grew accustomed to the semi-darkness Engelbrecht and I both saw the tail of the leopard protruding from behind the boulder. I had two rifles, one a Service ·303 which fired smokeless cartridges and which Engelbrecht was carrying and the other, which I was carrying, an old single-barrelled ·450 firing black powder cartridges. Engelbrecht said that if I would stand at the extreme right of the opening, he would fire at the tail which would make the leopard get up and give me the chance of a shot. When he fired, the tail did not move, but another leopard —obviously the wounded animal's mate—leapt out of the shadows and disappeared into the back of the cave. (He got out through a hole at the back of the cave.) The wounded leopard was growling so that we knew it was still alive. Engelbrecht then cut down a sapling and said that he would climb on to the boulder and poke the leopard out with the sapling so that I could get a shot at it. I protested that it was madness, but he said that we could not leave it now and I feebly gave way. We had with us three of the Game Watchers and I remember at this point suddenly catching sight of the three men each perched on the top of a small tree, looking down upon us with horror—and the sight did not reassure me.

Engelbrecht climbed on to the boulder: he was unarmed and he knew that I was about the worst shot with a rifle in the world. But he poked down at the leopard. At first there was only a burst of savage growls, and then suddenly the leopard sprang into view. I could see him quite clearly sitting up, slightly sideways, three or four yards inside the cave. I fired and jumped aside to the left in front of the boulder and Engelbrecht, Hodson, and I cowered down pressed together in the narrow space away from the opening. When I fired the whole cave was filled with smoke and out of the smoke a foot or two from us whizzed the leopard turning head over heels. He fell upon the rocks below, turned another somersault round another boulder, and there again was the end of his tail jutting out beyond the rock. Very very cautiously we crept down with our rifles ready and peered round the rock. He was dead; by a complete fluke, which I don't think I should have succeeded in bringing off once in twenty times, I had shot him through the heart.

I saw some remarkable sights in the Magampattu jungles. The Game Sanctuary itself was a fascinating place. Its western boundary was the Menik Ganga, a biggish river which, however, often had a mere trickle of water in it and only filled when there was heavy rain up country. I used to go and inspect the Game Sanctuary whenever I could spare the time, camping on the west bank of the river. West of the river where shooting was allowed, the game was as shy as everywhere else. As soon as you crossed the river into the Sanctuary, everything changed and you were in the Garden of Eden. Immense herds of deer, buffaloes before the rinderpest, pig, elephants roamed about in the open paying hardly any attention to you. The northern boundary of the Sanctuary was also the northern boundary of my District and the southern boundary of the Province of Uva; the eastern boundary was a river, the Kumbukkan Oya, which was the western boundary of the Eastern Province. The Game Watchers were expected to keep a broad track cleared all along the northern boundary, and on one of my circuits I decided to inspect the whole length of this to see that the work was really done. I camped on the side of the river and set out on foot early in the morning with Engelbrecht, ten Game Watchers, three coolies, and my dog-boy. It was a good two days' walk and we intended to spend the night in a cave. The coolies carried my camp bed and our food. That morning I saw something which I had been told sometimes happens in the jungle, but about which I had always been a little sceptical. We were walking single file along the track when some way ahead on the top of a small tree were eight or nine monkeys, chattering and shrieking, jumping up and down, up and down, their arms raised above their heads as if they were imploring heaven, their eyes fixed upon the ground. We crept slowly up to the tree and when we got quite near it, I heard from behind a big bush just under the tree click, click, click, click; it was a leopard clicking his teeth and when I fired through the bush, I saw him leap into the jungle and disappear. So the story was not a sportsman's yarn. The leopard lies under a tree on which he has seen monkeys and begins to click his teeth together. The monkeys get wildly excited and jump up and down, up and down with their arms above their heads and sooner or later one of them misses his footing, falls to the ground, and is eaten by the leopard.

In the afternoon it began to pour with rain. About six o'clock we got to some big caves and decided to spend the night there. It rained all night and was still raining in the morning. We were in a quandary, for, although when we left our camp the river was almost dry, the rain was so heavy that it would fill rapidly and if we did not hurry back to the camp we might find ourselves cut off from it for two or even three days by the river in flood. We turned back in pitiless rain. "The rain was wet," I recorded in my diary, "but the jungle was far wetter, and I think I was wettest. Most of the jungle was under water. In most places one walked in mud and water above the ankle, in many above the knee. . . . The last three miles was through a lake of mud with some firm patches. A cold bath in this district is often a luxury, but to stay in it for seven hours is excessive. I have never been colder than when we reached the dripping tents at Talgasmankada." In fact, we only just got back in time, for when we forded the river the water was up to our armpits and the stream running so strong that one kept on one's feet with difficulty.

But we were not by any means out of the wood. It rained heavily all night and in the early morning reached the tents. It was an amazing sight, a terrific flood sweeping down trees, the remains of huts, drowned cattle, buffaloes, deer. The roads were said to be so flooded as to be impassable to our carts so we decided to stay where we were. The river soon flooded the camping ground and we had to move everything into the Watchers' huts, already occupied by them and my two ponies. The river continued to rise and flooded the Watchers' huts, so that we had to abandon them, cut a path through the jungle, and pitch the tents on some high ground in an opening. Next morning I determined to try to push on at all costs and we started off at 6 a.m. The carts, with the water above the axles, took $6\frac{1}{4}$ hours to do $2\frac{1}{2}$ miles. We had some food in an open space at 1 and all round us the deer were out in the open as the jungles were flooded. We took the whole afternoon to do another $1\frac{1}{2}$ miles through water two or three feet deep. At Yala the watch station was under water and had been abandoned; the Watchers' families and their cattle were living on rough platforms made of sticks.

I saw two other rare sights in the Magampattu jungle. One day I had been out with one of the Game Watchers and was returning to my camp in the late afternoon. We suddenly came upon two bull elephants fighting. When we first saw them they were standing forehead to forehead pushing violently and playing a sort of ju-jitsu with their trunks, each trying, I think, to get its trunk round the foreleg of the other. After a time they backed slowly away from each other, and when they were separated by about 50 yards, they charged at full speed and met with a violent crash forehead to forehead. Then the pushing began again, followed again by a charge, and this went on for some time. It was a terrifying sight, this silent struggle of the two enormous beasts in a kind of arena of trodden grass, crushed bushes, and broken trees which they had

made with their tramplings and chargings. In the jungle
the wild elephant was always to me the most alarming
of all the animals. Coming upon him suddenly, as I so
often did, in thick jungle he seemed to me gigantic towering up above me; there is, too, something primeval and
malignant about him, his pachydermatous greyness, his
wicked little eye, the menace of his trunk, the slow,
relentless, ceaseless fidgeting. Coming face to face with a
buffalo, a bear, or a leopard one felt pretty sure of what he
would do, and in 999 cases out of a 1,000 one was right;
I never felt that I had any idea of what an elephant would
do: he might pay no attention to you at all or dash off in
a panic into the jungle or come lumbering after you.
Though I was terrified by the fighting bulls—and so, I
think, was the Watcher—we could not tear ourselves
away from the spectacle. We dodged about behind
bushes and trees watching sometimes only ten or fifteen
yards away from them, and always ready to bolt out of the
way when they backed from each other in preparation for
the charge. But suddenly one of them must have scented
us, for he stopped fighting and turned in our direction.
We made off as quickly as we could, and about two or
three hundred yards away we came upon a cow elephant
feeding peacefully.

I saw the other strange sight one day when I was out
with the same Watcher in thick jungle. We heard quite
near us the most extraordinary guttural roaring noise. I
had never heard it before and I asked the Watcher what
it was; he said that he did not know, he too had never heard
anything like it. We crept through the jungle towards the
sound and came to a small pool with a large dead tree
lying across it and on the tree lay an immense crocodile
making this strange roaring. The whole thing was dis-

quieting. A large crocodile, covered with slime and weeds, is more sinister and primeval than even the elephant; to see this creature lying flat on the dead tree, with his mouth wide open, and making this terrific choking roaring, was staggering. I shot him, and we then found that there was a large tortoise firmly stuck in his throat. I suppose that he had tried to eat it by breaking its shell and the tortoise slipped into the back of his throat; it was so firmly wedged that he would never have been able to get it out. He would have died a horribly lingering death—the jungle is a terribly cruel place.

It is difficult to know exactly why I found the jungle so fascinating. It is a cruel and a dangerous place, and, being a cowardly person, I was always afraid of it. Yet I could not keep away from it. I used to love going off entirely by myself—without Engelbrecht or the Game Watchers—and wander about ostensibly to shoot something for dinner, but really just to wander. I liked the complete solitude and silence and every now and again the noises which break the jungle's silence and which, as one learns its ways, tells one of the comings and the goings around one. For a few moments one had succeeded in getting oneself out of the world of one's fellow men—which I always do with a sigh of relief—into a world of great beauty, ugliness, and danger. The beauty was extraordinary and you never knew behind what tree or bush or rock you might not suddenly see it. You slink slowly round a rock in thick jungle and there in a small opening are five or six dazzling peacocks. I once climbed up a large rock, about 40 or 50 feet high, in the middle of the jungle, and standing on the top was a superb sambhur deer, his antlers silhouetted against the sky. When he saw me, he went off down the rock at full speed, and, when he was half-way down, he just launched himself out into space, falling with a crash on bushes or small trees, and disappeared into the jungle. It was a magnificent sight, the great deer with his forelegs and hind legs flat out and his antlers flat on his back catapulting himself off the rock into the air. Another time on a game track I turned a corner and there in the fork of a tree twelve foot from the ground hanging over the branch was the body of a full-grown stag, and on the body lay a leopard eating it. We stared at each other for a moment, and then the leopard just poured himself off the tree as if he were made of elastic or even some miraculous fluid, and disappeared into the jungle.

This kind of beauty of wild animals I never get tired of. But the jungle and jungle life are also horribly ugly and cruel. When I left Ceylon, and wrote *The Village in the Jungle*, that was what obsessed my memory and my imagination and is, in a sense, the theme of the book. The more you are in jungle, particularly if you are alone, the more one tends to feel it personified, something or someone hostile, dangerous. One always has to be on one's guard against it or against—one never quite knows what. I twice lost myself in jungle, a terrifying experience, and each time it was due to carelessness, to forgetting for an instant to be on one's guard against the treachery of the jungle. The first time was only for ten minutes or a quarter of an hour, but it gave me a nasty jar. I often had to go from Hambantota town to Tissamaharama to deal with irrigation, cultivation, and judicial work there. My carts went by road, but there was a track through the jungle which one could ride on and cut off about 12 miles of the cart road. I nearly always rode by this track. At one point I used to dismount, tie my pony to a tree, and push my way through 200 or 300 yards of thick jungle north of the track into an enormous open clearing, circular, about half a mile or more in diameter. One used sometimes to see deer, peafowl, or jungle fowl in it and that was why I used to go there. One day I did this and, after roaming about for five or ten minutes, decided to go back to my pony. I had not noticed that the sky was overcast. When I turned to go back, I could not find the place at which I had entered. Normally when the sky was clear all I had to do was to enter the jungle, go due south, and I would soon strike the track on which I had left the pony. Now I was faced with a circle of jungle a mile or more round this open space, and the wall of trees and leaves was exactly the same all round the circle—and I could not tell which was south and which north. I tried again and again to creep and crawl 200–300 yards through the jungle, first in one place and then in another, but I could not strike the path. It is a golden rule in jungle, when you want to find your way back exactly to the place you started from, to break twigs and boughs as you pass, which will guide you back on your return journey. I had carelessly neglected to do this because the distance was so short. But, although the distance was so short, I was hopelessly lost for there was no means of knowing in which direction the track lay. However, after trying again and again, and marking the places where I had already tried, I at last thought I heard my pony some distance off, as I was crawling under the thorn bushes. And so it was.

The other time I lost myself was even more idiotic and unpleasant. When I went to Tissa, I sometimes used to start after I had done a day's work in Hambantota and spend the night at Weligatta circuit bungalow eight miles along the Tissa road in order to get to Tissa as early as possible next morning. My carts and servants went by road and I rode, cutting across country through scrub jungle. One evening, when I was doing this, I arrived at the bungalow before the carts. I tied my pony to a tree and went off into the jungle north of the bungalow. I had often seen peafowl in the neighbourhood and I thought I would try to find the big trees on which they roosted. I moved about rather aimlessly for half an hour and then decided to go back to the bungalow. I knew exactly how the road and the tracks ran and that, if I walked due west, I would come out either dead on the bungalow or a little to the north of it on the Tissa road or a little to the south of it on a path to a village, Bundala. I also knew that I had already crossed and would have to recross a fairly distinct game track running north–south. It was not long to sunset; I was in thick jungle, and I set off towards the light of what I took to be the setting sun.

After slow progress through thick thorn jungle for about a quarter of an hour, I came to the conclusion that something was wrong, because I had not crossed the game track and the jungle was much thicker and thornier than it was in the neighbourhood of Weligatta. I climbed a tree and found that I had made a fool of myself. There had been a heavy rainstorm, and the western sky was still covered with a black cloud, the eastern sky was bright with reflected light from the west. I had been walking due east instead of due west; I was now in dense jungle, with a great deal of impenetrable thorn bush, and I was probably three-quarters of an hour's walk from the bungalow; there was probably another ten minutes of daylight. I made a push for it, but after five minutes it was clear that I had not a chance of getting out before it was dark. The

jungle was soaking wet and so was I. I had a copy of the
rinderpest regulations in my pocket and a matchbox with a
few matches in it. I decided that I would light a fire under
a big tree while there was still light and resign myself to
a night in the jungle.

It was only with my last match that I got the damp
paper and damper wood to start a bonfire. I built up an
enormous fire, but it was really an extremely unpleasant
night. To keep a fire going for 8 or 9 hours requires an
immense amount of wood. I can sleep anywhere and I
slept on the ground close up to the fire, but every hour I
had to wake up and forage about for more wood. It was a
wearisome business and there was considerable danger
from snakes as one fumbled about in semi-darkness—
there was no moon—for wood. I got so sick of it that at
3 o'clock in the morning, having satisfied myself about
the points of the compass from the stars which I could
glimpse through the trees, I decided to start back for the
bungalow. I built up an immense fire so that I would be
able to return to it if I failed to get through. After five
minutes I found it impossible in the darkness to get
through the dense thorn bushes, but when I tried to find
the fire, it was invisible. I had to lie down and sleep where
I was. The sun woke me and it took me just under an hour
to get out walking due west and coming out of the jungle
within two hundred yards of the bungalow. I found my
servants and villagers and headmen in a great state over
my disappearance. The only effect upon me was a more
than usually severe attack of malaria.

The instinct for direction or the "homing" instinct is
very mysterious and variable. I noticed that with the Game
Sanctuary Watchers it varied enormously. Some of them
were not really very good at finding their way instinctively

back through the jungle to the last place where we had camped. On the other hand there was one Watcher who, at any moment anywhere, could stop and go straight back to the exact spot he had left five or six hours ago in thick jungle. In Chapter Two I gave an example of the homing instinct of my horse; I had a still more extraordinary display of it with a dog in Hambantota. I bought a bitch, a half-bred hound, from an advertisement which a planter up country had put in the newspaper. When the bitch was delivered to me, she had obviously been very badly treated and was terrified of me and everyone else. After a week she suddenly realized that I was never going to beat her and she attached herself to me as no other dog has ever attached itself to me. She had a puppy whom I called Mermaid. When Mermaid was about three months old, I decided that the time had come when she could come out on circuit with me. Up to that time she had never been more than, say, half a mile from the bungalow, taken along the road for a walk with the other dogs morning and evening by the dog-boy. I had at this time three other dogs besides Mermaid, and one Friday evening I rode out with the four of them across country to meet my carts eight miles away at Weligatta where I proposed to spend Friday and Saturday nights. The first six miles or so was through scrub jungle and then one came out of the jungle on to a great dry lagoon about a mile long. Mermaid followed admirably with her mother and the two other dogs through the jungle. When we got out on to the sand of the lagoon, the pony began to gallop and started off in front of us a great herd of cattle. Before I knew what was happening cattle, dogs, and pony were tearing and thundering across the lagoon in the wildest excitement. We must have gone a quarter of a mile in this mad way when I suddenly remembered Mermaid, pulled up the pony, and was horrified to find that she was not with us. She must have been frightened by the thundering of hoofs on the sand and bolted back into the jungle. I went all round the edge of the jungle searching and calling for her, but she had completely disappeared and when it became dark I had to abandon the search. I gave up all hope of her for, as I said, she had never been more than at most half a mile from my bungalow, the jungle was thick scrub, and she would probably be soon picked up by a leopard. I stayed Saturday at Weligatta and went back late on Saturday afternoon to Hambantota. At nine o'clock in the evening, after dinner, I was sitting reading on the verandah when suddenly out of the darkness there shot a white body and Mermaid hurled herself into my lap. She was dead beat, lame, bleeding from scratches; she had taken over 24 hours to find her way back through a pathless jungle and then—what must have been even more confusing and terrifying for her—the town of Hambantota.

The District, as I have said before, was famous for its big game shooting and in the open season a considerable number of white people, both residents in Ceylon and visitors to the island, came and applied for licences to shoot elephant, buffalo, and deer. As time went on and my experience of the jungle, shooting, and shooters increased, I became more and more prejudiced against my fellow white men. I may have been sometimes over-severe. Engelbrecht reported to me once that two planters, to whom I had issued licences to shoot deer, had shot deer in the river bed which was the boundary of the Game Sanctuary. I issued summonses upon them and had them brought up before me in Hambantota before they could leave the District. After enquiry it was clear that one of them had shot a deer in the bed of the river. I told him what I thought of him as a "sportsman" and said that, quite apart from that, I considered that the bed of the river was within the Sanctuary and I proposed to prosecute him for shooting within the Sanctuary. I could try him as Police Magistrate, but if he objected to being tried by me, I would get another P.M. appointed to try his case and would let him know the date of the trial. But if he would rather have the case dealt with by me on the spot, I said I would fine him Rs. 50. He was extremely angry, but he eventually paid the fine and departed.

I found the international "sportsmen" even more uncongenial. Before the Crown Prince of Germany visited Ceylon, the Governor sent his A.D.C. down to Hambantota to discuss with me whether I advised his coming to my District to shoot. I managed to get out of this, but I had some curious experiences with royal and aristocratic sportsmen. Big game shooting was organized in Colombo as big business. The would-be hunter or party went to a Colombo firm which undertook to provide them at Hambantota with bullock carts, trackers, tents, food and to organize the shoot for them. The sportsmen came to me for licences and a strange company they were. One Sunday morning when I was working in my bungalow my boy brought me three cards and said that three gentlemen wanted to see me. A Prince, a Duke, and a Count came into my room: one was a Bourbon, one an Orleans, and one a Napoleon. I issued licences to them. In the afternoon I happened to see the expedition start from the town. There were four bullock carts. The two in front contained an immense number of boxes, tents, and furniture. The third was empty, and walking beside it were the three sportsmen. The fourth contained a bevy of ladies who seemed to me most unsuitable for the jungles of Magampattu; their normal place of domicile was, I guessed, a Colombo brothel.

One day I received from the Government in Colombo a telegram informing me that Baron Blixen, a Danish cousin of Queen Alexandra, was coming to shoot in my District, and I was to help him in every way possible. I found that the Baron was one of a party of Scandinavian aristocrats who were coming to shoot. Two days later the party arrived and their leader Count Frijs called on me, accompanied by his daughter. The Count was a tall, very good-looking Swede; the Countess made my heart, chaste and chastened by two years in Hambantota, turn over in my breast. She was the dream Scandinavian Countess of the glossy woman's magazine and of the unsophisticated (or indeed sophisticated) male heart. About 21 years old, she had the yellowest of corn-coloured hair, the bluest of sky-blue eyes, the most delicate, soft, rose-petal pink complexion. And they were charming, with all the charm and perfect manners of the aristocrat who wants to get you to do something for him. What they wanted of me was first to give them licences to kill a large number of wild animals, and secondly to look after Queen Alexandra's cousin when he arrived in Hambantota. For Baron Blixen was not with them; he had become slightly unwell in Colombo and would not be well enough to come to Hambantota for a day or two. The Count, his lovely daughter, and the rest of his party proposed to set off at once to the jungle and begin their shoot; the famous Herr Hagenbeck of Colombo—famous in the world of zoos and circuses—would in a day or two bring the Baron to Hambantota and hand him over to me, and would I have

219

the great goodness to take charge of the Baron and bring
him to Count Frijs?

I promised Count Frijs that I would do what he asked
of me and they departed for the jungle in a shower of
thanks and smiles. I had to go to Tissamaharama to hold
an enquiry, and I left directions for Herr Hagenbeck and
the Baron to be sent on to me there. They arrived in a
motor-car two or three days later. Baron Axel Blixen was
a middle-aged man with mutton-chop whiskers, watery
eyes, and a distant resemblance to the Prince Consort. He
was extremely nervous, and, holding my hand in his two
hands, besought me not to leave him alone in the jungle,
but take him and hand him over to Count Frijs. I reas-
sured him, but, as they had made no arrangements where
to meet the rest of the party, I had to send out messengers
in various directions to try to find them. Meanwhile
Baron Blixen had to spend the night with me in the Tissa
Rest House. In the late afternoon I asked him whether he
would like to shoot something; we could either go out in
the Irrigation Engineer's punt on to the tank just before
sunset and shoot teal, or I would take him round the tank
and give him a shot at a crocodile. He chose the crocodile.
We set off round the tank and after about half a mile I
pointed out to him a large crocodile lying by the water's
edge about 30 yards from us. The Baron took careful aim
and fired, and his bullet hit the ground less than 15 yards
from his toes and more than 15 yards from the crocodile's
toes. Next day a messenger arrived with a note saying that
Count Frijs was at Palatupana, and, having delivered
Baron Blixen there, I returned to Hambantota, once more
in a shower of smiles and gratitude. Some two or three
weeks later the party returned to Hambantota, and the
Baron came up to see me. He had had a most successful

shoot and he asked me to come and see his trophies. His shooting had improved enormously since the evening at Tissa. I cannot now remember exactly what he showed me, but certainly several deer and I rather think a bear. His terror that I should abandon him in the Ceylon jungles before he found Count Frijs may, of course, have affected his shooting, though I have never seen anyone else, even myself, make quite such a bad shot. I should add that the Baron was an extremely kindly and courteous man. One of my mother's sisters had married a Dane and lived in Copenhagen. When Baron Blixen got back to Denmark with his trophies, he called upon my aunt, told her about his meeting with me, and was enthusiastically grateful for all that I had done for him.

I do not know how the Baron came to shoot so badly at Tissa and so well at Palatupana. But I know that it was a common practice for the tracker supplied by the Colombo organizer of the expedition to stand by the sportsman's side, particularly in the case of a dangerous animal like a bear or buffalo, and shoot at the same moment as the sportsman. A great deal of this big-business organized safari or whatever they called the thing in Colombo was despicable butchery. The most contemptible "sport" was the shooting of elephants; I used to take every excuse to refuse licences to shoot an elephant, and I un-successfully tried to get the Government to make a regulation that the A.G.A. should stop the issue of licences, except in the case of a particular elephant in a particular place which he was satisfied was either a rogue or was habitually causing damage to crops.

As time went on, I became, I think, more and more severe and unrelenting, particularly in relation to my fellow white men, and this sometimes got me into hot water. One incident, in which I still think that right was in the main on my side, had, I heard, a bad effect upon my reputation among some people who never heard my side of the happening. Whenever I was in Hambantota town, I used to bathe in the evening in the bay. There was a very ancient, derelict jetty, the top of which was quite sound and was six or eight feet above the sea. From the end of it, there had once been a flight of steps down to a landing stage, but the wooden steps and platform had long ago disappeared and only an iron skeleton, covered with barnacles, remained. I used to dive from the jetty itself into the sea, but to get out on to the iron skeleton of the landing stage required great care, agility, and experience. The only safe way was to swim quietly up to it and allow a wave to lift you up above it so that, as the wave fell, your two arms were left supporting you on the iron girder and you could then gingerly get your feet upon the girder, avoiding the lacerating barnacles. There was always a fairly heavy swell rolling into the bay. I am not a very good swimmer but continual practice had taught me exactly how to get out of the sea on to the girder. One day a civil servant, whom I will call X, came to Hambantota for a night on some business and stayed with me. He said he would like to bathe in the evening; I explained how I got out of the water, but asked him not to try to do it, unless he was a first-class swimmer, and instead to come back to the shore. When I had got out on to the jetty after our swim, he began to follow me and I implored him not to do so, but to swim straight back to the shore. He would not do so, and being a heavy, fat man, he was soon in difficulties and his legs and arms bleeding from the barnacles. I really thought he was going to drown and went back into the water to help him swim to shore. It was an extremely unpleasant experience, for he was exhausted and we were swept together under the jetty. I only just got him and myself to the shore.

About three months later another civil servant, whom I will call Mr. Y, came for a night and stayed with me. We went down to bathe; I told him of my experience with Mr. X and said that he must not on any account try to get out of the sea on to the jetty; if he did so and got into difficulties, I should let him drown for I was not going to repeat the very unpleasant experience of rescuing Mr. X. Mr. Y did exactly what Mr. X had done and was soon in great difficulties. I refused to go in to help him, and eventually, having swallowed a great deal of sea-water, exhausted and angry, he struggled ashore. I too was angry, especially when I heard that it was being widely said that I had behaved in a cowardly and ruthless way to Mr. Y. Nothing was ever said about Mr. X.

I also got into hot water with my superiors, particularly the Government Agent, C. M. Lushington. I thought Lushington to be a rather stupid man and prejudiced against me as being too young for my post and "jumped up" by Sir Hugh Clifford. Shortly after I was made A.G.A. he recommended the appointment of a headman in my District without consulting me, a very unusual proceeding. I protested to Government, recommended someone else, and won my point. He several times opposed innovations which I introduced or recommended, and here again once or twice I got my way against him. No doubt I was arrogant and offensive, and he had a good deal to complain of against me. At the end of my time in Hambantota, in fact just after I went on leave, I was sent by Lushington a copy of the following letter which he had received—I am sure with great pleasure—from the Colonial Secretary:

19th May, 1911
Colonial Secretary's Office
Colombo.

Sir,

I am directed to request you to inform Mr. Woolf that His Excellency the Governor has observed that the tone of his comments in his diary and in endorsement No. 205 of 26th April to the Government Agent, Southern Province, regarding the acquisition of land required for the Public Works Department Store at Tangalla, leaves much to be desired.

2. His Excellency accordingly desires you to instruct him to comment with more restraint and discretion upon the orders of his Superior Officer.

I am, etc.

A. N. Galbraith
for Colonial Secretary.

In my last year at Hambantota, and as the time for my leave came nearer and nearer—I was due for a year's leave at the end of 1910 but, owing to the Government's difficulty in finding a successor, had to wait until May 20th, 1911—I became more and more doubtful about my future. What may be called the imperialist side of my profession had become consciously distasteful to me. If I was very successful in my career, as I now was certain I should be, I would be promoted sooner or later to the Central Government and Colombo, and would go on to become a Colonial Secretary and Governor. The prospect filled me with despondency though the temptation of power and position was felt by me. Not for the last time, confronted with a choice of worldly goods or paths, I thought of the French poet:

HAMBANTOTA

Si le roi m'avoit donné
Paris sa grand' ville
Et qu'il me fallût quitter
L'amour de ma vie!

Je dirois au roi Henri
Reprenez votre Paris;
J'aime mieux ma mie, o gué,
J'aime mieux ma mie.

And, of course, just as the Paris which the world offers
you and tempts you with is not always the same, ranging
from perhaps a Governorship at one moment of your life
to an editorship or what is called security at another, so
l'amour de ma vie and *ma mie* are not always the same.
The *ma mie* for which I was prepared to sacrifice Paris was
in one case no doubt Virginia, but it has also been occasionally in my life a kind of independence or freedom
denied to you in Civil Services and similar occupations
which bring you pomp and power.

On the other hand I became completely immersed, not
only in my work, but in the life of the people. The more
remote that life was from my own, the more absorbed I
became in it and the more I enjoyed it. In July, 1910, I
had to go and superintend the famous Kataragama Pilgrimage. Kataragama was not actually in my District; it
was a tiny village in dense jungle in the Uva Province, but
it had no roads to it and was so far from any inhabited
place in Uva that it was practically inaccessible to the
G.A. of that Province. It was about ten miles from Tissamaharama and the A.G.A. Hambantota always had to
look after it. It was a very curious experience. The pilgrimage, which took place every three or four years, was

225

famous in Ceylon and all over Southern India. In the old days great numbers of pilgrims used to come from India. They trailed along the south coast of Ceylon through Galle and Matara into the Hambantota district. From Hambantota town to Kataragama there were practically no villages and neither food nor shelter was obtainable. Among pilgrims there are always a large number of sick people who are brought to the temple to be cured by the God. These unfortunate people trailed along the un-populated Magampattu road and along the jungle track from Tissa to Kataragama, half starved, many of them falling sick and dying on the way. There was something even worse than this: very often they brought with them from India cholera or smallpox, and the pilgrimage more than once was the cause of serious epidemics in Hamban-tota which spread through the island. Eventually the Government made strict regulations for the pilgrimage. It was allowed only at intervals and no one was allowed to come to it except on a ticket issued by the Ceylon Government. A limited number of tickets were sent to the Government of India to issue to would-be Indian pil-grims and a certain number were reserved for people in Ceylon. I had 75 tickets and 300 applicants.

I rode to Kataragama from Tissa in the early morning of July 8th and I stayed there 14 days, until July 22nd when the pilgrimage ended. There were between 3,000 and 4,000 pilgrims. Many of them were town dwellers who had never seen a jungle. They had travelled by sea and train to and through a strange land; men, women, and children had trudged 180–200 miles along the roads and on the jungle track to find themselves dumped for a fort-night with three or four thousand other people in a clear-ing in dense jungle. For Kataragama in 1910 was little

more than a large clearing in the unending jungle. It had
two temples, one at one end of what might euphemisti-
cally be called the village street—it was only a very broad
path between boutiques and sheds—and the other at the
other end. The religious set-up of the temples and the
pilgrimage was most confusing. The temples were Hindu
and the priests were Tamil Hindus; the Managers
were Sinhalese Buddhists. Buddhists as well as Hindus
came to the pilgrimage, and low caste people, dhobies
and pariahs, were allowed into the temple, which would
never be allowed in an ordinary Jaffna Hindu temple.
Every evening the image of the God was carried in procession to the other temple—a kind of juggernaut procession with the pilgrims following or rolling over and
over in the dust before the God's car. In the other temple
was the God's wife or concubine and after visiting her he
returned to his own temple. On the last day of the festival
the priest and all the pilgrims went to the river with the
image of the God, and there, standing in the middle of
the river, the priest "cut the waters" with a knife—and
the festival was over.

One day during the festival I climbed the Kataragama
hill, a pretty high rugged hill some distance through the
jungle from the temples. It took me four hours' strenuous
walking and climbing, but I got a fine view from the top
of the miles and miles of jungle stretching to the Uva and
Batticaloa hills and mountains. A Sinhalese villager came
with me to show me the way and we got talking about the
God and the temples. According to this Sinhalese the
Kataragama Deviyo (God) was Kandeswami and originally had his temple on the top of the Kataragama hill.
One day he thought he would like to cross the river and
live in Kataragama. He asked some Tamils who were

passing to carry him across. They said that they were on the way to Palatupana to collect salt and could not do so, but they would carry him across on their way back. A little while afterwards there came by some Sinhalese and the God asked them to carry him across the river into Kataragama. They did so at once. The God at that time was a Tamil, but he married into a Sinhalese family in Kataragama and became a Sinhalese God, and that is why now the temple kapuralas are Sinhalese. This was the story of a Buddhist Sinhalese villager. When I told his story to my servant, a Hindu Jaffna Tamil, he said that that was "all tales": the God is Kandeswami and no one else. But he could not explain how the dhobies and pariah are allowed into the temple if it is really a Hindu Kandeswami Koyil.

The only really bad sleepless night I can remember to have had in my life was in the village of Kataragama. The pilgrimage is a kind of Ceylon Lourdes, and hundreds of sick people dragged themselves or were dragged through the jungle to be cured by the Kataragama Deviyo. My bungalow—the only one in the village—was just above the temple. The pilgrims used to spend the night round the temple and one night when I went to bed, a child was screaming and crying in a terrible way in the courtyard of the temple just below my room. After a bit, I could not stand it, called my boy, and told him to go down into the temple and ask the parents either to do something to pacify the child or remove it from immediately under my window. My boy returned, but the child went on crying and it cried all night, "in the night, with no language but a cry", a terrible, unending, tortured cry. I felt in my bones that it was no good doing anything more; my boy would have had the thing stopped if he could; there was

something behind it which I would learn in the morning.
So I lay awake hour after hour tortured by the tortured
howling of the child. In the morning I asked my boy
what it all meant. He was very sorry, he said; the people,
a mother and father, had come from India with the child.
The child was blind, and they had come to Kataragama
to ask the God to give him sight. The God had not heard
their prayers and they thought that perhaps if they made
the child cry long and loud enough, the God would hear
him. They had therefore pinched the child and had even
pricked him with pins to make him cry. I went down to
the temple and found the parents. They were South Indian
villagers, unhappy, tired, bewildered; the child was blind.
I asked them whether they would come with me and let the
District Medical Officer, a Sinhalese, look at the child's
eyes. They agreed, for they were resigned to agree to
anything. According to the D.M.O., there was nothing
that he could do. The child was blind and neither Kandeswami nor science could give him sight.

It was these kind of strange, alien psychological en-
counters which fascinated me—the mixture of pathos and
absurdity, of love and cruelty, in such horrible and
grotesque incidents. I ought to have hated my 14 days
supervising the pilgrimage. The heat during the day
makes life intolerable; I wrote at the time, "one cannot
exist in the bungalow after 10 a.m. without wearing a hat
of some sort while the glare is enough to warrant smoked
spectacles. In this condition one sits in a perpetual sand-
storm waiting for the sun to go down and for the mosquitoes to come out and take the place of the eyeflies. I
hope that the Kataragama God sees to it that the super-
visor of the pilgrims acquires some little merit from this
pilgrimage." Yes, despite the physical miseries and the

complete isolation, I enjoyed my fortnight and left
Kataragama with slight regret. The complete self-confidence of the British imperialist in 1910 was really rather
strange. Here was I, an Englishman aged 29, who had
collected in the middle of the Ceylon jungle nearly 4,000
men, women, and children, gathered together from all
over Ceylon and Southern India. I was responsible administratively for everything connected with the well-
being of these people and for the maintenance of law and
order. If anything had gone wrong during the pilgrimage
I should have been blamed. But we were so firmly convinced that, if one white civil servant was there, nothing
could possibly go wrong, that I had no staff and no police.
I had the District Medical Officer to look after the health
of 4,000 people and the village headman to maintain order
among them. Our self-confidence was fully justified. I had
little or nothing to do except to answer questions, listen to
complaints, keep an eye on what was going on, particularly during the processions. In the early morning or late
afternoon I used to take my gun and wander off alone into
the jungle and down to the river, and I was able to find
out a good deal about the illicit shooting of deer and a kind
of large-scale traffic in dried meat which, I had long
known, went on all along the northern boundary of my
District. I enjoyed the meditative isolation of my pilgrimage to the Kataragama Deviyo.

Sometimes the good that men do is not interred with
their bones, it lives after them to be turned into evil.
When the pilgrimage was over I wrote to the Government
Agent and recommended that the Government should
make the Kataragama temple authorities provide accom-
modation for the pilgrims. I pointed out that the
authorities got between three and four thousand pilgrims

to come to Kataragama and the revenue which they obtained from offerings must have been pretty considerable. There was not cover enough in the village to shelter 1,000 people; there had been heavy rain during the pilgrimage and the result was much malaria and pneumonia. The authorities, I said, should at least provide temporary cadjan buildings and cut drains round them.

I left Kataragama on July 23rd, 1910. I saw it again on my visit to Ceylon on February 16th, 1960. The jungle track from Tissa had been converted into a good road over which I was comfortably driven in a car. My recommendation had certainly been carried out, but the Kataragama that I knew had disappeared. There was now a large car park by the side of the river and a bridge over the river; there was now shelter for the pilgrims. There were many things connected with the Kataragama of 1910 which were evil and which to me were repellent. I dislike superstition wherever I find it, whether among primitive and simple people or sophisticated ninnies. But at least there was something fundamentally genuine, primitively real there in the jungle. The people believed what they believed simply and purely. The beliefs were deplorable, no doubt, but the purity, simplicity, and their motives for taking the terrible journey to the temple I respected. Even the temple authorities, though they were, like most Church authorities, greedy and disingenuous, seemed to have some faint belief in what they preached or professed. The pilgrimage was an authentic, spontaneous explosion of the hopes and aspirations of ordinary men and women who lived hard and bewildered lives. The Kataragama of 1960 is the exact opposite. Like Lisieux and other famous European places of Christian pilgrimage its whole atmosphere is that of the commercialized exploitation of credulity. Walking up what was before the village street, you passed boutique after boutique, selling flowers and fruit, to be offered in the temple and *mutatis mutandis* you might have been passing the shops in Lisieux or even in London's Victoria Street, selling their candles and images of the Blessed Virgin. I went into the temple, where in 1910 I had often gone to talk about arrangements for the procession with the priest, in order to see what things were like in 1960. I took the usual offering of fruit and flowers, but was advised that the offering would not be received by the God unless a rupee, as a minimum, was included. When I saw the priest—I have seen his spit and image in many cathedrals, churches, and temples—I had no doubt that he was the God's financial adviser. The only thing which he was interested in was my rupee which he abstracted at once. What surprised and saddened me was to find that even educated Sinhalese would drive all the way from Colombo to Kataragama to worship in this temple, despite or because of its commercialized religion.

In the last half of my time in Hambantota I had, I think, an extraordinary wide and intense knowledge of the country and the people. If a man came into the kach-cheri or the Court, more often than not I could tell from his looks which village he came from. The knowledge was indeed reciprocal; if the A.G.A. knew the people, the people got to know the A.G.A. Many of them did not like his severity. I always encouraged the headmen and villagers to talk quite freely to me. One day, camping in a village in West Giruwa Pattu, I had a crowd of petitioners who kept me at work until the evening. When the enquiries were over, I stayed talking to them for a bit. Halley's comet was blazing in the sky. The villagers informed me that they did not like the comet and that it was an evil age for the people. The village headman then gave me the following list of evils which had come upon them:

(1) the road tax,
(2) the V.C. tax,
(3) the irrigation rate,
(4) the taxes on carts and guns,
(5) the restriction of chenas,
(6) a strict Assistant Government Agent.

He invited me to take as my model a previous Assistant Government Agent who had allowed chenas freely and, when he left the District, wept among weeping headmen.

When I visited Ceylon again after 50 years I had a curious instance of the long memory of grievance and of my severity. Hardly any of the headmen or government officers who had worked under me were alive. But on my last day in Colombo, a man who had been chief headman of one of the pattus when I was A.G.A. came to pay his respects to me at the Galle Face Hotel. After desultory conversation, he suddenly said to me: "Do you remember, Sir, when you made me shoot the buffalo?" I said no, I did not remember it. "You heard", he said, "that there were stray buffaloes, affected with rinderpest, in the village of Liyangahatota, and you sent a message to me to meet you in the village with the village headman. We found the buffaloes in a large stretch of paddy field, and saw that one of them was badly diseased. When we tried to get near them, they ran off. Then you told the Arachchi to go and drive the sick buffalo down the field to you so that you could destroy it. The Arachchi said it had gone savage and would attack him. You insisted, but when he got near the animal, he became afraid and ran away. Then you gave me your gun; you were riding a horse and you said that you would go and drive the buffalo down to me and that I was to shoot it. This we did. Then you asked who owned these buffaloes and why had they been allowed to stray? It turned out that it was the Arachchi himself who owned the buffaloes. You fined the Arachchi 10 rupees for not carrying out his duties as headman and not seeing that the buffaloes were impounded. Then, as Police Magistrate, you tried him as owner of the buffaloes for allowing a diseased animal to stray and you fined him 25 rupees. Ten days later the man came to me with 20 rupees to pay his fine, but he could not pay the other 15 rupees and I had to pay it for him. It was too severe, Sir—was it fair, Sir, was it fair?" After 50 years I felt I could not be quite certain of the answer. *Was* it fair?

For some time in 1910 I was bombarded with anonymous and pseudonymous letters, all in the same handwriting, abusing me and threatening me. They were the result of two incidents. Information about what was happening or going to happen in the District used to reach me from many different sources, often unsolicited. I was told—very confidentially—that in a latrine that I was having built in the town the work was being done in a most dishonest way with the connivance of the Government officer responsible. What should have been solid cement according to the estimate was rubble with a very thin coating of cement. When it was reported that the building was completed and certified by him as properly built according to specification, I told him to meet me at the place with a pickaxe. He fell on the floor in a faint. When I examined the building it proved to be a complete swindle and the Government officer was dismissed. I had a suspicion that the anonymous letters came from his father.

The other incident in which the same family was involved was more interesting. Gambling was illegal in Ceylon, partly because it often led to violent crime and disorder. One day I came back from circuit to Hambantota town a day earlier than expected and I was told by someone that about 100 strangers had come to the town from all along the south coast, even from Galle and Matara, far outside my District, for organized gambling, and that my Police Sergeant was conniving. I made arrangements with someone other than my informant to let me know at once if gambling began again. Two nights later after midnight a message came to say that the gambling was going on. The following entry in my diary describes what happened:

I sent word to Mr. Doole, Mudaliyar of East Giruwa Pattu, whom I had instructed to remain in Hambantota for the purpose, to keep watch and inform me of a favourable opportunity as watchers were said to be "keeping cave". At 1.30 a.m. Mr. Doole came to my bungalow and told me that gambling was going on in two houses. At 2 a.m. we got to the first and after sending men round to the back door I went on to the verandah. Eight persons were gambling and one was lying asleep on a couch. Among them were the Police Sergeant himself, the Vidane Arachchi of Tissa, and the Mudaliyar's clerk. It was an extremely diverting sight to see their faces when I put my head in at the door. I prosecuted them all except the Sergeant in the Gansabhawa this morning and they were fined. I am dealing with the Sergeant departmentally.

It was, of course, depressing to find that one's severity was much resented and anyone who tries to insist that a large number of persons, particularly government servants, shall work hard and efficiently, is bound to be unpopular. On the other hand, my vanity was flattered because it seemed to me that, as time went on, in many ways the people seemed to trust me more and came to me to settle their disputes and solve their difficulties. It was in this kind of work that I became most deeply absorbed. There was, for instance, a large village in the extreme west of the District in which a tremendous dispute over the ownership of land had been going on for a long time and had caused an immense amount of litigation and even some crimes of violence. The whole thing was characteristic of village life in Ceylon 50 years ago. The kernel of the trouble was 48 acres of land, the ownership of which was in dispute between the villagers on one side and the Court interpreter of Tangalla on the other. When I went to the village, both sides agreed to submit the matter to me for arbitration. I held the enquiry in the village, sitting from 8 in the morning to 4 in the afternoon in the middle of a crowd of about 250 excited partisans. I decided that 18 acres belonged to the interpreter and 30 acres to the villagers. But I had become convinced that as long as the interpreter owned any land in the village, there would be trouble, and I induced him to agree to sell and them to buy the 18 acres. It then became necessary to assess the price to be paid. After $5\frac{1}{2}$ hours of strenuous negotiation I got the villagers to agree to pay Rs. 5,000 in two annual instalments. But if I thought that that settled the dispute, I was very much mistaken. First of all the whole thing broke down because the villagers began to quarrel among themselves as to how the land was to be distributed among them. I refused to accept defeat and went down again and again to the village, enquiring minutely into the claims to ownership. It took me six months to get 44 people to agree to my decision as to who should be the owner of 44 lots and to my assessment of what each should pay to the interpreter for his lot. They then actually, to my astonished relief, deposited Rs. 5,051 to be drawn by the interpreter when the deeds were executed. Then other difficulties arose involving more enquiries and negotiations, and it was another six months before all the parties met in my presence and the deeds were signed and the money paid over.

Another big dispute which I settled interested me greatly. There was in Hambantota town a mosque and quite a large number of Moslems, chiefly Malays. I knew that a great deal of ill-feeling had arisen among them, when the Hakim died, over the selection of a successor. Some of them wanted Mr. Doole, a chief headman, to be appointed, others wanted a Mr. Bahar who was the Government Salt Superintendent. I was rather concerned by the growing ill-feeling, but it was very difficult for me to interfere. Then one day a card was brought in to me and I was told that a gentleman wished to see me. The gentleman proved to be a rather melancholy, but tough-looking Englishman. He said that his name was Hadji Salam Robertson; he had been an officer in the Leicestershire Regiment, but just after getting his company he was converted to Muhammadanism, had resigned, and had made the pilgrimage to Mecca. He was travelling through the East and went from place to place lecturing on the Moslem religion, the lore and law of which he had studied deeply. He was going to give a lecture in Hambantota and he and the local Muhammadans wanted me to take the chair. I agreed to do this provided that the local Muhammadans confirmed the invitation. I told him about the Hakim dispute and asked him to try to get the rival factions to agree over an appointment. He said that he would do so, but that if they could not agree, the right procedure was for them to remit the dispute to Constantinople for settlement.

The lecture took place; it was interesting and nearly all the Moors and Malays attended, but I noted at the time that I rather doubted whether they understood much of it. But, to my surprise, shortly after it the leaders of the two factions came to me and asked me to try to settle the dispute. I found it to be a curious and rather dangerous situation. There were two mosques in the town, one old, and one new. A section of the Muhammadans whom they called Karawas or Fishers had been excommunicated from the old mosque and they had built a new mosque of their own. Mr. Doole was the leader of the old mosque party and Mr. Bahar of the Fishers. I arranged for the rival leaders and the trustees of the two mosques to come to my house. It was clear from the discussion that the ordinary people were quite ready for a settlement and would choose a Hakim acceptable to both parties—it was the leaders who would not agree. I could not induce them to accept a compromise but I made it clear to them that I would not allow the formation in Hambantota of two dangerous factions headed by two of the chief Muhammadan Government officers. They went away and two rival Hakims were elected, which was quite irregular. Some time later I received a letter from Mr. Doole saying that there would be a serious disturbance at the mosque at next Friday prayers. Mr. Bahar and the Fishers had announced their intention of praying at the old mosque and Mr. Doole and his party were going to resist them: every man had been told to come "taking one sandal in the hand". Two hundred and fifty men were assembled on one side and 150 on the other. Everything seemed to be prepared for very serious trouble. I sent for the leaders, talked frankly to them, explaining to them exactly who would be held responsible if there were a disturbance. I told the Government officers concerned that, as they had roused up the people, I should hold them personally responsible to calm them down. I noted in my diary that "the warning was sufficient and it was not necessary to fall back upon the police force of Hambantota which consists of one sergeant." In fact a few days later the leaders again asked to see me. We had a meeting and after prolonged discussion a settlement was proposed to which they said all would agree. Three days later it was announced that the Hakim dispute was ended.

These were sophisticated disputes among sophisticated people, and they were dangerous because they might easily have led to large-scale violence. What fascinated me more were the queer problems and disputes which quite often the unsophisticated villagers put before me. For instance, one day noticing a man who looked rather ill, I asked him what was the matter with him. He said he was suffering from "yak leda", which means devil sickness. How, I asked him, did he catch devil sickness. Well, he said, one night he went to look at the wells, which he was in charge of, and in the dark he ran against what he thought was a devil. It turned out to be an old woman, but he had been ill with devil sickness ever since.

In a remote village on the coast a curious female trade existed. The village women used to swim out 300 yards from the shore, dive down, and fish up big coral stones.

They swam back with the stones and stacked them in heaps called fathoms, 6 foot by 6 foot by 6 foot. The stones were sold for building purposes at Rs. 4 to Rs. 6 per fathom. The output was about 300 fathoms a year and I was told that as many as 2,400 women work off and on— a number which seemed to me quite incredible. When I went to see the diving, the women told me that they never got malaria. One day when I was passing near the village, a large deputation of the women stopped and asked me to help them. The stones which they had fished up had been seized by the Forest Department on the ground that they were "forest produce". I wrote to the Assistant Conservator of Forests that I did not think that even the law, which everyone knew was an ass, could include the sea in the legal definition of a forest. The Assistant Conservator of Forests released the stones from seizure.

It was very rare for village women to put their problems before one. I had in fact, I think, only one other case. One day on circuit in a rather remote part of the District I was riding along a path when I was stopped by a number of women belonging to the Berawaya or tom-tom beater caste with a strange request. By immemorial custom they were not allowed to wear jackets; the most that they were allowed for covering of their breasts was a narrow strip of cloth which they wound over their breasts and under their armpits. They asked my permission to wear jackets, giving as their reason that they could not pound rice decently owing to this strip of cloth. I told the petitioners that it was not for me to tell the Sinhalese women what clothes they could or could not wear, but that I would have a talk with the village headman. I knew the Vidana Arachchi to be a crusted conservative, and I had small hope of his agreeing to any change. At first he said that the tom-tom beating caste had never been allowed to wear jackets, but, after some discussion and cogitation, he said that if the women did not put their arms into the sleeves, they might be allowed to wear jackets just hanging round their necks. I told the women that they had better do this and they were quite satisfied; I felt sure, that after another 50 years, the Berawaya women's arms would be in the sleeves. But one had to be careful about caste customs and demands to change them. I once had to help the police quell a serious riot in Jaffna which arose in the following way. When a high caste man died, his corpse was carried out of his compound to cremation or burial not through the gate, but part of the cadjan fence was torn down and the corpse was carried out through the hole. Suddenly one of the lower castes announced that they would follow the same practice and the higher caste objected. When a man of the lower caste died and the corpse was about to be carried out, a large crowd of the higher caste gathered outside the house and when the dead man's relations began making a hole in the fence a fight began. There were soon a hundred or more men fighting savagely on the road and in the compound. Before we got to the scene and stopped the fighting, a dozen men had been seriously injured.

The nicest case which I was ever asked to settle was in a large village of West Giruwa Pattu called Walasmulla. I was holding enquiries and also conducting a sale of Crown Land situated in a neighbouring village. I was surrounded by a large crowd of villagers. Suddenly in the middle of the proceedings the crowd parted and an old man with one side of his face shaved and the other unshaven rushed into the ring and fell at my feet. He complained that the barber in the bazaar (and he was apparently the only barber in Walasmulla), after shaving one side of his face, had refused to shave the other unless paid 50 cents. The correct price of a shave in Walasmulla was 5 cents. I sent for the barber and he appeared accompanied by some hundreds of spectators. After enquiry, I told the barber that he must complete the shave and he would be paid nothing, but if he cut the old man, he would have to pay him 50 cents. The old man was in deadly earnest, but the barber, who had the face of a rogue and a humorist, appeared to be greatly amused. We adjourned to a coconut tree in the compound of the Rest House and there the operation of shaving the old man was completed before me and an enormous crowd of spectators. The spectators were obviously delighted and amused and this revealed a characteristic of the Sinhalese which always endeared them to me. The relations between Europeans and some Asiatic peoples are made difficult because the Asiatic does not seem to share the European's sense of humour. This is not the case with the Sinhalese. They are a humorous people and they have the same kind of sense of humour as the European. Even in a remote village I felt that I could make a joke which would be appreciated.

Just before I left Hambantota an incident occurred which proved—what I knew only too well—that one never knew what might not happen and that, even in the quietest place, peace was precarious. There was very little crime in Hambantota town and the police force consisted, as I have said, of one Police Sergeant. During my three years there the various races and religions had lived amicably side by side. But a night or two before I left, when I was taking my dogs for a stroll near my house, a man came running towards me shouting: "Come, Sir, quick—they are killing one another in the town. Come, Sir, quick." We ran as hard as we could to the town and on the way he told me that the Buddhists and Moslems, armed with sticks and stones and with the posts which they pulled out of the fences, were fighting one another in front of the mosque. When I got to the spot, I found a large crowd of angry people, but the fighting was practically over. A number of Sinhalese Buddhists were being besieged in a house by angry Moslems. There were six or seven Moslems wounded and covered with blood and one Sinhalese, a Government servant, who lived near the mosque, had tried to stop the row when it began, and had been hit by a stone in his face. I was immediately surrounded by a crowd of people telling me different stories. I noticed three or four people who, I was sure, were not residents of the town and would therefore be more or less unbiased. So I got hold of them and took them straight away, accompanied by most of the combatants, to the Police Court. I had the Court opened and by the light of lamps began at once to record evidence.

It was soon quite clear what had happened. There had been a Buddhist procession through the town. Because they might easily result in religious disturbances, religious processions with tom-toms were not allowed except on licence. The licence prescribed through what streets the procession might go and always contained a clause forbidding the beating of tom-toms while the procession was passing a place of worship belonging to a different religious community. In this case the row had begun when the Buddhist procession, contrary to the terms of the licence, beat their tom-toms while passing the mosque. Some Moslems tried to stop this and the Buddhists fell

upon them and severely handled them. The Moslems in
the bazaar, hearing what was happening at the mosque,
rushed to the spot in large numbers, tearing up the fences
as they came in order to provide themselves with weapons.
The Buddhists, seeing that they would be overwhelmed,
sought sanctuary in the house where I had found them
being besieged.

This, of course, was not quite the story told to me in
the witness-box by the strangers, who were themselves
Buddhists and Sinhalese. But as they had no time to get
together with their co-religionists and prepare their
evidence—which was my object in starting proceedings at
once—they very clearly gave it all away. After recording
sufficient evidence to show beyond doubt what had happened, I adjourned and went to bed. Next morning the
leading Moslems and Buddhists came to see me, and the
following entry in my official diary shows what happened:

The leaders on both sides wished to settle the matter of
yesterday amicably. No one had been seriously hurt.
There has also never been any religious feeling in the
town and there is no doubt that, if cases with proctors
on each side had been engaged on, such feeling would
be engendered. I therefore said that if the persons
responsible on each side would plead guilty to charges
which I would frame against them I would allow the
cases of hurt &c. to be withdrawn. This was done and
I fined one side for disturbing a religious procession
and the other for tom-toming without licence, the
Muhammadans Rs. 35 and the Buddhists Rs. 60. The
penalties were, of course, light, but as a matter of
expediency much will have been gained by allowing the
religious ill-feeling to die out at once.

My last day in Hambantota, I spent visiting the schools. I had built and opened a Government Tamil school in the town and had made primary education compulsory. Father Cooreman, a Belgian Roman Catholic missionary, had a Sinhalese school in the town. I visited these two schools and the last entry in my diary records that "the numbers have gone up very well since we began to enforce attendance and there are signs of some knowledge being driven into the heads of the youth of Hambantota."

Next day I departed for Colombo, and from Colombo, with my sister Bella, now married to the Assistant Director of the Peradeniya Gardens, I sailed for England.

Chapter Five

EPILOGUE

OUR boat left Colombo on May 24th, 1911, and arrived at Marseilles on June 10th. We took the train across France and next day, Sunday June 11th, got back to London. I went and stayed with my family at Putney, for my mother and brother and sisters were still living in the house to which we had migrated from Kensington nearly 20 years before. What I found in England and my life in London after June, 1911, belongs to the third volume of my autobiography, if I ever write it. Here I am merely concerned with the ending of my life in Ceylon.

When I got to London, I was still in the doubt about my future which I have referred to in the last chapter. But I had a year's leave before me and I decided to dismiss the whole matter from my mind for at least six months and enjoy myself. I did enjoy myself. I found my Cambridge friends living in or about Bloomsbury: Lytton Strachey, Saxon Sydney-Turner, Virginia and Adrian Stephen, Vanessa and Clive Bell, Duncan Grant, Maynard Keynes. After Jaffna, Kandy, and Hambantota, the Prices and Lewises, Gwen and Rachel it was a plunge— a slightly icy plunge—into an entirely different world, almost a different universe. But I was received by them all as one of themselves and slipped without much difficulty into the kind of place which I had occupied in 1904 when I sailed for Ceylon. And yet perhaps not entirely the same, for I think the seven years in Ceylon left a mark

upon my mind and even character which has proved in-
delible, a kind of reserve or withdrawal into myself which
makes me inclined always to stand just a little to one side
of my environment. But for a time I did dismiss Ceylon
from my mind. I saw a great deal of them all and went to
the Russian Ballet and the *Ring* with them, and dined
with Vanessa and Clive and with Virginia and Adrian, and
stayed with Virginia in a house which she rented in Firle
near Lewes. And I went up to Cambridge, and stayed
with Moore and Lytton on Dartmoor.

In the autumn Virginia and Adrian took a large house
in Brunswick Square. They let the ground floor to
Maynard Keynes and they offered to let the top floor to
me. I agreed and in December went into residence there.
I had been feeling for some little time that I must make a
decision about Ceylon. In October I began writing *The
Village in the Jungle* and I realized that I was falling in
love with Virginia. By the end of 1911 I had come to the
following conclusions: (1) If Virginia would marry me, I
would resign from Ceylon and try to earn my living by
writing; (2) If Virginia would not marry me, I did not
want to return to Ceylon and become a successful civil
servant in Colombo and end eventually with a governorship and K.C.M.G. But if I could go back and immerse
myself in a District like Hambantota for the remainder of
my life, as Dyke and old Sir William Twynam had immersed themselves in Jaffna, I might welcome it as a final
withdrawal, a final solitude, in which, married to a Sinhalese, I would make my District or Province the most
efficient, the most prosperous place in Asia. At the back
of my mind I think I knew that this last solution was
fantasy. The days of paternalism under a Dyke or Twynam were over; I had been born in an age of imperialism

and I disapproved of imperialism and felt sure that its days were already numbered.

In May my leave would be up. So in February, being still in doubt about the future, I decided to try to get my leave extended. On February 14th, 1912, I asked the Secretary of State for the Colonies to extend my leave for four months. I received from him the following letter:

Downing Street,
16 February, 1912

Sir,

I am directed by Mr. Secretary Harcourt to acknowledge the receipt of your letter of the 14th February applying for an extension of your leave of absence from Ceylon; and to request that you will be so good as to state the nature of the private affairs to which you refer.

I am, Sir, your obedient servant

H. J. Read
for the Under Secretary of State

I replied that I could not state the nature of my private affairs, and the following correspondence then continued to its destined end:

Downing Street,
29 February, 1912

Sir,

I am directed by Mr. Secretary Harcourt to acknowledge the receipt of your letter of the 20th February with regard to your application for an extension of your leave of absence.

2. Mr. Harcourt regrets that he is unable to grant you an extension without a more explicit statement of the nature of the private affairs to which you refer than

is contained in your letter under acknowledgment. This explanation may, if you wish, be given in a confidential letter which will not be communicated to the Government of Ceylon, except in so far as you may agree to its being communicated to the Governor confidentially.

3. If, however, you would prefer not to state the exact nature of the private affairs, Mr. Harcourt will ask the Governor whether an extension can be granted to you on the ground of service, without making any reference to the reasons for which you desire it.

I am &c.

H. J. Read

for the Under Secretary of State

To the Under Secretary of State   1 March, 1912

Sir,

I have the honour to acknowledge receipt of your letter of 29 February.

2. I should prefer that the course proposed in paragraph 3 of your letter under reply should be followed, i.e. that the exact nature of the private affairs be not stated and His Excellency the Governor be asked whether an extension can be granted to me on the ground of service.

3. I have the honour to submit that unless my private affairs absolutely necessitate it, I do not desire to prolong my leave and that if circumstances subsequently permitted of my leaving England before the expiration of the four months extension now applied for, I would immediately report the fact to you so that, if desired, I might then resume my duties.

I am &c.

Leonard Woolf

From the Under Secretary of State

Downing Street
23 April 1912

Sir,

I am directed by Mr. Secretary Harcourt to inform you that the Governor of Ceylon has now reported that the extension of absence for which you applied cannot be granted.

2. Mr. Harcourt, therefore, regrets that he must call upon you to resume your duties at the end of the leave already granted to you, which expires on the 20th May.

I am &c.

G. V. Fiddes

To the Under Secretary of State
Sir,

With reference to your letter of 23rd April I have the honour to report that as I am unable to assume duties on May 20th I regret that I must resign my post under the Ceylon Government from that date.

I am &c.

Leonard Woolf

From the Colonial Office (in handwriting)

29 April, 1912

Dear Sir,

I am desired to write to you with regard to your letter of the 25th and to say that, before accepting your resignation, Mr. Harcourt would like to give you an opportunity of reconsidering the question.

In accordance with your wish, the Governor of Ceylon was only asked whether you could be given an extension of leave "on the ground of service." He has

replied that this cannot be done and it is of course
impossible for Mr. Harcourt to overrule him. The
grant of leave on the ground of urgent private affairs is,
however, another matter and is one for the decision of
the Secretary of State.

If, as would appear from your letters, your private
affairs make it impossible for you to return to Ceylon
at present, Mr. Harcourt, on being satisfied as to their
urgency and importance, would probably be prepared
to grant you an extension. If, however, you are still unwilling to state the exact nature of these affairs, Mr.
Harcourt will have no alternative but to accept your
resignation.

It is for you to decide whether you will now state
their nature. If you do so by letter, the matter will be
absolutely confidential and, if an extension is granted,
the Governor will only be told that the leave is granted
on the ground of private affairs, the nature of which
has been explained to the satisfaction of the Secretary
of State. Or if you are unwilling to state them in
writing, do you care to come and tell me about the
matter in person? Anything you tell me will go no
further. It will only be necessary for me to report that
I am satisfied that there is proper ground for granting
an extension.

Yours faithfully,
R. E. Stubbs.

I did not feel that I could explain to Mr. Harcourt or
Mr. Stubbs that I had come to dislike imperialism, that I
did not want to become a Governor, that I wanted to
marry Virginia Stephen, and that, if I didn't marry her, I
would like to continue to be a Ceylon Civil Servant pro-

vided that they would appoint me permanently Assistant
Government Agent Hambantota. I merely thanked him
for his letter and said that my resignation must stand,
murmuring to myself as I signed the letter:

> *Mr. Secretary Harcourt,*
> *Reprenez votre Paris;*
> *J'aime mieux ma mie, O gué,*
> *J'aime mieux ma mie!*

To which Mr. Secretary Harcourt replied:

Downing Street,
7 May, 1912

Sir,

I am directed by Mr. Secretary Harcourt to acknowledge the receipt of your letter of the 25th April, in
which you tender your resignation of your appointment in the public service of Ceylon.

2. Mr. Harcourt understands that you are not prepared to accept the suggestion which has been made to
you privately that you should state confidentially the
nature of the urgent private affairs on account of which
you desire an extension of your leave of absence, in
order that the question of granting you an extension
might be considered. He regrets, therefore, that he has
no alternative but to accept your resignation which will
take effect from the 20th May.

I am &c.

H. J. Read
for the Under Secretary of State

INDEX

INDEX

Books by Leonard Woolf
available in paperback editions
from Harcourt Brace Jovanovich, Inc.

SOWING: AN AUTOBIOGRAPHY OF THE
YEARS 1880 TO 1904

(HB 319)

GROWING: AN AUTOBIOGRAPHY OF THE
YEARS 1904 TO 1911

(HB 320)

BEGINNING AGAIN: AN AUTOBIOGRAPHY
OF THE YEARS 1911 TO 1918

(HB 321)

DOWNHILL ALL THE WAY: AN AUTO-
BIOGRAPHY OF THE YEARS 1919 TO 1939

(HB 322)

THE JOURNEY NOT THE ARRIVAL MATTERS:
AN AUTOBIOGRAPHY OF THE YEARS
1939 TO 1969

(HB 323)

––––––––––––––

FIVE-VOLUME BOXED SET

(HB 324)